How the Grace of God Can Take You ...

From BAD BEGINNINGS
To HAPPY ENDINGS

HOW THE GRACE OF GOD CAN TAKE YOU...

From BAD BEGINNINGS *To* HAPPY ENDINGS

ED YOUNG

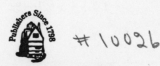

Publishers Since 1798

THOMAS NELSON PUBLISHERS
Nashville • Atlanta • London • Vancouver

Published in Nashville, Tennessee, by Thomas Nelson, Inc., and distributed in Canada by Word Communications, Ltd., Richmond, British Columbia, and in the United Kingdom by Word (UK), Ltd. Milton Keynes, England.

Scripture quotations are from the NEW KING JAMES VERSION of the Bible. Copyright © 1979, 1980, 1982, Thomas Nelson, Inc., Publishers.

Scripture quotations noted NASV are from the NEW AMERICAN STANDARD BIBLE, copyright © 1960, 1962, 1963, 1968, 1971, 1972, 1973, 1975, 1977 by The Lockman Foundation and are used by permission.

Library of Congress Cataloging-in-Publication Data

Young, H. Edwin, 1936–
    [Against all odds]
    From bad beginnings to happy endings / Ed Young.
       p.   cm.
    Originally published: Against all odds.   c1992.
    ISBN 0–7852–7952–0
    1. Family—Religious life.   2. Family.   3. Joseph (Son of God)
I. Title.
    [BV4526.2Y67   1994]
    248.4—dc20   94–9587
                                                                                 CIP

Printed in the United States of America
1 2 3 4 5 6 7 — 99 98 97 96 95 94

To
"Goosie" and "Little Goose"

For my granddaughter, Lee Beth, and my grandson, E. J., it is my prayer that they and their families in succeeding generations will incorporate these biblical principles into their lives, and will prove over and over again the timeless truth and dependability of God's Word.

Preface

Throughout my ministry God has given me a special concern for and commitment to the strengthening of families on the basis of God's principles. Certainly not a day goes by that I do not thank Him for my own family—my wife, Jo Beth, our three sons, Ed and Ben—who are married now, and Cliff, our youngest, who is a college student. Also, I am grateful for the "daughters"—Lisa and Elliott—that Ed and Ben have married and brought into our lives. They have enriched our "all boy" household after so many years. And then, of course, there are the wonderful "crowning touches" that He has given to us in our granddaughter, Lee Beth, and our grandson, E. J. The fresh, exciting joy they bring to our lives each day could only come from a loving Heavenly Father.

In my mind there is no question that Jo Beth is the inspiration and heart of our Christian home. To be sure, I have sought to be the leader/lover of the family, but it is my selfless mate who has sacrificially poured into her four men the love that made the difference in our lives. She has "kissed and tucked in" all the Youngs, night after night, for 32 years. The fruit of the Spirit is clearly evident in her life—she makes our home sizzle!

Not only am I grateful for our immediate family and for the legacy handed down to us from past generations, I am also grateful for the church families God has allowed us to be a part of through the years. During the last fourteen years, so many members of the Second Baptist family have made a difference in our lives, and their prayers and friendship have sustained and encouraged us in countless ways. I especially want to thank those church members who allowed me to use their stories in this book. Their real-life struggles and victories will inspire and encourage many with new hope.

My medium is the spoken word. I write to speak and do not speak to write. Therefore, the transition from pulpit to paper was a tedious and difficult one. Split infinitives, mixed metaphors, dangling participles, and "three-mile-long" sentences had to be eliminated. Four long-suffering associates accomplished this task. So I want to thank Beverly Gambrell for diligently tracking down a wealth of information and detail in the preparation of the sermon series that became the basis of the book you now hold. Early in the process, Laura Kates spent long hours turning the spoken word into written text, and her efforts are deeply appreciated. Linda Richard provided not only administrative support, but many editorial suggestions that made this a more readable book in the end.

And finally, Leigh McLeroy was really the prime mover in this writing assignment. She expanded, clarified, wrote and rewrote, and made sense out of many long, homiletical meanderings. I am especially grateful to Leigh for the tremendous job she did in combining all the integral parts of a sermon series on the story of Joseph, and in bringing to life a manuscript that prayerfully will prove—unequivocally—not only for Joseph, but for each one of us as well, God's principles *always* work.

Contents

Chapter 1

Kissed and Tucked In

Beating the Odds

*The LORD was with Joseph, and he
was a successful man . . .*
Genesis 39:2

Kissed and Tucked In

A young man cowered in the corner of a dirty, roach-infested death row cell in a South Carolina prison. His body curled in a fetal position, he seemed oblivious to the filth and stench around him. His name was Rusty, and he was sentenced to die for the murder of a Myrtle Beach woman in a crime spree that left four people dead.

Police arrested twenty-three-year-old Rusty Welborn from Point Pleasant, West Virginia in 1979, following one of the most brutal slayings in South Carolina history. Rusty was tried for murder and received the death penalty for his crime. Bob McAlister, deputy chief of staff to South Carolina's governor, became acquainted with Rusty on death row. Bob had become a Christian a year or so earlier and felt a strong call from God to minister to the state's inmates—especially those spending their last days on death row.

Bob's first look at Rusty revealed a pitiful sight. Rusty was lying on the floor when he arrived, a pathetic picture of a man who believed he mattered to no one. The only signs of life in the cell were the roaches who scurried over everything, including Rusty himself. He made no effort to move or even to brush the insects away. He stared blankly at Bob as he began to talk, but did not respond.

During visit after visit, Bob tried to reach Rusty, telling him of the love Jesus had for him and of his opportunity—even on death row—to start a new life

Rusty was lying on the floor when he arrived, a pathetic picture of a man who believed he mattered to no one.

in Christ. He talked and prayed continuously, and finally Rusty began to respond to the stranger who kept invading his cell. Little by little, he opened up, until one day he began to weep as Bob was sharing with him. On that day, Rusty Welborn, a pitiful man with murder and darkness behind him and his own death closing in ahead of him, gave his heart to Jesus Christ.

When Bob returned to Rusty's cell a few days later, he found a new man. The cell was clean and so was Rusty. He had renewed energy and a positive outlook on life. McAlister continued to visit him regularly, studying the Bible and praying with him. The two men became close friends over the next five years. In fact, McAlister said that Rusty grew into the son he never had, and as for Rusty, he had taken to calling McAlister "Pap."

Bob learned that Rusty's childhood in West Virginia had been anything but "almost heaven." His family was destitute, and Rusty was neglected and abused as a youngster. School was an ordeal both for him and for his teachers. Throughout his junior high years he wore the same two pair of pants and two ragged shirts. Out of shame, frustration, and a lack of adult guidance, Rusty quit school in his ninth grade year, a decision that was to be just the beginning of his troubles. His teenage years were full of turmoil as he was kicked out of his home many times and ran away countless others. He spent the better part of his youth living under bridges and in public rest rooms.

Bob taught Rusty the Bible, but Rusty was the teacher when it came to love and forgiveness. This young man who had never known real love was amazed and thrilled about the love of God. He never ceased to be surprised that other people could actually love someone like him through Jesus Christ. Rusty's childlike enthusiasm was a breath of fresh air to Bob, who came to realize how much he had taken for granted, especially with regard to the love of his family and friends.

In time Rusty became extremely bothered by the devastating pain he had caused the family and friends of his victim. Knowing that God had forgiven him, he desperately wanted the forgiveness of those he had wronged. Then a most significant thing happened: the brother of the woman Rusty had murdered became a Christian. God had dealt with him for two years about his need to forgive his sister's killer. Finally, he wrote Rusty a letter that offered not only forgiveness but love in Christ.

Not long before his scheduled execution, this brother and his wife came to visit Rusty. Bob was present when the two men met and tearfully embraced like long-lost brothers finally reunited. Rusty's senseless crime ten years earlier had constructed an enormous barrier between himself and the brother. The love of Christ obliterated that barrier and enabled both men to realize that, because of Him, they truly were brothers reunited on that day. It was a lesson Bob would not forget.

Not only did Rusty teach Bob McAlister how to love and forgive, he also taught him a powerful lesson about how to die. As the appointed day approached, Rusty exhibited a calm and assurance like Bob had never seen. On his final day, with only hours remaining before his 1:00 A.M. execution, Rusty asked McAlister to read to him from the Bible. After an hour or so of listening, Rusty sat up on the side of his cot and said, "You know, the only thing I ever wanted was a home, Pap. Now I'm going to get one."

Bob continued his reading, and after a few minutes Rusty grew very still. Thinking he had fallen asleep, Bob placed a blanket over him and closed the Bible. As he turned to leave he felt a strong compulsion to lean over and kiss Rusty on the forehead. A short time later, Rusty Welborn was executed for murder. A woman assisting Rusty in his last moments shared this postscript to his story: As he was being prepared for his death, Rusty looked at her and said, "What a shame that a man's gotta wait 'til his last night alive to be kissed and tucked in for the very first time."

Does it seem almost unbelievable to you that a convicted killer—a man who had brutally murdered an innocent woman with little or no thought

> *A*fter an hour or so of listening, Rusty sat up on the side of his cot and said, "You know, the only thing I ever wanted was a home, Pap. Now I'm going to get one."

for the consequences—would mourn the fact that as a child no one kissed him, no one tucked him in? That is a tragedy. Each one of us is born with the need to be loved. The first love many of us receive (or believe we have an inherent right to receive) is the love of our parents. The family is the structure through which this love is administered, but today it often fails to provide that first nurturing love and the absence of it is too often felt far into adulthood.

A loving happy home was not a part of Rusty Welborn's childhood. But what if he had been "tucked in" as a child? What if loving parents had read him a story, then gently kissed his forehead each night before turning out the light? What if they had told him they loved him? Would things have turned out differently? Can a person ever hope to overcome the obstacles created by broken homes and bad beginnings? You won't have to read to the end of this book to find out that I believe the answer to that question is a resounding yes!

*B*roken homes and toxic families are not unique to our modern society. In fact one of the greatest men in all the Bible came from a home that was full of conflict and severely lacking in discipline.

Broken homes and toxic families are not unique to our modern society. In fact one of the greatest men in all the Bible came from a home that was full of conflict and severely lacking in discipline. His name was Joseph, and his story illustrates many of the things that can and do go wrong in families today. His beginning was in the land of Canaan, where his father, Jacob, and his mother, Rachel, lived. As beginnings go, it was a fine one. His mother gave birth to him later in life, after she and his father had prayed many years for him. So many, in fact, that his father's other wives (his aunt Leah, Bilhah, and Zilpah) had already had several children!

He loved his mother and she loved him. His brothers always said he was his father's favorite, and they were probably right. But when he was just a boy Rachel died, and their home life after that was unusual even by Bedouin standards. Twelve boys with four different mothers and a father who loved them, but did not lead them. It was an environment ripe for conflict, and they had their share. The competition that naturally exists between siblings was intensified in their home as he and his brothers vied for their father's attention, time, affection and inheritance.

He left home earlier than he had planned. (Actually, he had never planned to leave home at all, but more about that later.) Suffice it to say he was forced out of the nest a bit prematurely, and he landed in a culture totally foreign and unfamiliar to him. He started over many times in his life. This was to be just the first of many changes. Wherever he found himself, he tried to make the best of his circumstances. Regardless of the way things looked, he always believed that God (the God of his father, his father's father, and his father as well) had a purpose for his life. This he never forgot. Even though it happened thousands of years ago, the elements of his story resurface each day in homes across modern America.

But Joseph, as we'll see in the pages ahead, had two crucial things going for him. First, he was loved. As the long-awaited child of two people who married for love, Joseph was welcomed into his family with excitement and gratitude. I believe his parents, especially his mother, let him know early on how much he was loved. Although she died when he was still a child, she was certainly able in those first few years to "kiss and tuck in" her precious son.

It is impossible to overestimate the value of a parent's love in a child's life. There is no adequate replacement for the parental attention children crave; not even lavish gifts or possessions showered on an otherwise forgotten child can compensate for a lack of parental love. Studies have shown its absence to affect nearly every facet of a child's nurture, from

> *Wherever he found himself, he tried to make the best of his circumstances. Regardless of the way things looked, he always believed that God had a purpose for his life.*

academic performance to sexual identity. Children need nurturing, and without it they struggle.

Second, Joseph lived with a constant awareness of the presence of God in his life. When he was a young boy, God gave him dreams that set his life on course and filled him with hope and purpose. He had dreams you wouldn't believe (or maybe you would), but they caused him no end of trouble from the very start. When he shared them with his brothers they were overcome with jealousy and came to hate him.

But Joseph never forgot the visions, even in his darkest days. They sustained him, encouraged him, and ultimately delivered him many times and in many places. When all around him seemed chaotic, he remembered those dreams. They gave him purpose and significance and reassured him that God did have a plan for his life.

As a child, the dreams (and his immature handling of them) had a negative impact, but as Joseph grew into adulthood he found strength in them. They became his "terrible good"—a fearful thing deep within him that was in fact a tremendous gift for great good.

Nature or Nurture?

Joseph faced incredible obstacles to growth and success and yet became a key figure in the eventual establishment of the nation of Israel. He had every reason to fail but he didn't. He was kidnapped and left for dead, sold as a slave, exalted, imprisoned, used, forgotten, and feared. He saw many changes through the years, and also discovered one constant: nothing in life is more real than the presence of God. God was the one thing in his life that never varied. Many people might have given up in circumstances similar to his, but they would have missed the thrill of the unfolding of God's plan.

He had crippling strikes against him, but prospered in the long run because he knew what it felt like to be loved. In every trying circumstance he clung to the belief that God had a special purpose for his life.

Psychologists have debated for years whether heredity or environment plays the stronger role in shaping the human personality. The "nature vs. nurture" argument has continued in one way or another for decades. Some would contend that we are chiefly products of our heredity, that our parents and our biological background have the greatest influence over who we become. Others hold that the environment we live in plays the primary role in determining our personality and our destiny.

In Joseph's case the environmental cards seemed stacked against him: He was the product of a broken, divided home, motherless at a young sensitive age and saddled with a doting but ineffective father who indulged him continually, and hated by his step-brothers. Yet this young man grew to become perhaps the godliest man in the Old Testament—a man of strength, wisdom, and character unlike any other, with the possible exception of the prophet Daniel.

No matter what drama we have been cast in as a character, it is possible to "re-script" what has been written for us and live a story that is uniquely our own.

Perhaps in Joseph we find the real truth about the heredity or environment issue: It's not nature or nurture that determines our destiny—it's neither! No matter what drama we have been cast in as a character, it is possible to "re-script" what has been written for us by heredity or environment and live a story that is uniquely our own.

Writer Ernest Hemingway, whose novels *The Sun Also Rises*, *For Whom the Bell Tolls*, and *A Farewell to Arms* are an integral part of our American literature, was the son of devout Christian parents. His writing was forceful, action-packed, and often brutal but exhibited none of the belief his parents tried to instill in him. Hemingway professed a concern with "truth," but his truth bore little resemblance to Christian principles modeled by his parents while he was growing up. Early in his life, he rejected these principals as irrelevant.

A letter from his mother written in 1920 illustrates how completely he had divorced himself from their beliefs: "Unless you, my son, Ernest, come to yourself, cease your lazy loafing and pleasure seeking . . . stop trading on your handsome face . . . and neglecting your duties to God and your Savior Jesus Christ . . . there is nothing for you but bankruptcy; you have overdrawn."

Hemingway told a writer for *Playboy* magazine in 1956 that "What is immoral is what you feel bad after." By his own standard, then, he was a man of unimpeachable morals—nothing made him feel bad. "People with different ideas about morality would call him a sinner," the article continued, "and the wages of sin, they say, is death. Hemingway has cheated death time and time again to become a scarred and bearded American legend, a great white hunter, a husband of four wives, and a winner of Nobel and Pulitzer prizes. . . . Sin has paid off for Hemingway."

Ten years later, in a review of the book *Papa Hemingway* by A. E. Hotchner in the same magazine, the account of Hemingway's life is a chronicle of repeated suicide attempts, paranoia, multiple affairs and marriages, and finally, on his return to his Ketchum, Idaho hideaway, his final—and successful—suicide attempt. How haunting and ironic the words written earlier about this man became. Ultimately sin did indeed pay off for Ernest Hemingway.

Our family's faith does not automatically become our own faith. Hemingway's parents were professing Christians who tried to rear their son according to their beliefs. But just as surely, the weaknesses of our families do not automatically become ours either. A childhood like Rusty Welborn's does not guarantee a wasted life. Without question we are responsible for the choices we make as thinking adults, and we, not our parents, will be held accountable for them.

Getting Past the Scars

Many adults attempt to blame their shortcomings or failures on events that took place in childhood, as though their experiences were unique. No one escapes childhood without scars. Our parents did not, we did not, and our children will not. We all have scars! The man or woman who ultimately becomes the person God intended is not someone without scars but one who has allowed Jesus Christ to "break the power of canceled sin" and to heal and use these unique marks of experience.

The missionary poet Amy Carmichael saw scars in this same light—not as hindrances but as evidence of identity with the Savior:

> Hast thou no scar?
>
> No hidden scar on foot, or side, or hand?
>
> I hear thee sung as mighty in the land,
>
> I hear them hail thy bright ascendant star,
>
> Hast thou no scar?
>
> Hast thou no wound?
>
> Yet I was wounded by the archers, spent,
>
> Leaned me against a tree to die; and rent
>
> By ravening beasts that compassed me, I swooned;
>
> Hast thou no wound?
>
> No wound? No scar?
>
> Yet as the master shall the servant be,
>
> And pierced are the feet that follow me;

The man or woman who ultimately becomes the person God intended is not someone without scars but one who has allowed Jesus Christ to "break the power of canceled sin" and to heal and use these unique marks of experience.

But thine are whole, can he have followed far
Who has not wound, nor scar?[1]

Completely Forgiven and Delightfully Whole

Recently AIDS claimed the life of a young member of our church. Three years before his death he had accepted Christ and walked away from a deep involvement in the homosexual lifestyle that had kept him on an emotional roller coaster since childhood. Sexual abuse, distorted and damaged family relationships, and a deeply wounded self-image were all part of the hurt and confusion Richard (not his real name) finally gave to Jesus.

While he was reared in a Catholic home and attended parochial schools, he had never really understood and responded to the message of the gospel. Later in life, his work as an interior designer brought Richard in contact with a wide variety of people, including another designer who was a Christian and persistently but lovingly shared her faith with him. He began attending our church a short time after this and walked the aisle one Sunday after praying to receive Christ. (His rendition of this miraculous story was even more engaging when he told it in his colorful Cajun drawl.)

Not long after he surrendered his life to Christ, Richard tested positive for HIV. This crushing news could easily have made him bitter, but it didn't. While others might have questioned God's love in these circumstances, Richard was so grateful for his new life in Jesus Christ that he didn't want to waste a minute of it in self-pity or regret. Instead he viewed every day as an opportunity to tell someone the good news he had discovered about God's complete forgiveness. No one was overlooked: street kids, designers, waiters, busboys, clients, suppliers, and old friends from his former lifestyle were a captive audience for this vibrant young man's witness.

Even with the scars from his childhood and the choices he had made as an adult, Richard was a walking testimony of the grace of God. Until he became too ill to continue, he ministered to others struggling with homosexuality and repeatedly echoed the witness of a loving God who could not only heal, but miraculously make all things new. Many of these individuals were greatly encouraged by his testimony, and his impact on their lives continues even today. He was a real life picture of one who allowed God not only to heal his life, but to use the scars of his past for great and eternal good.

Richard's health was unaffected by the AIDS virus for nearly three years. Soon after his thirtieth birthday, however, he began to be plagued by a series of physical problems, none of which were initially life-threatening. But in the all too familiar manner of this horrible disease, his immune system began to deteriorate and his ability to ward off various infections virtually disappeared. Even though his many friends prayed for months for Richard's healing, he died three months after his first hospitalization.

Richard's funeral service was a gathering of the most eclectic group of people imaginable. But they all had one thing in common: They loved him, and he had loved them. After the music and prayers were done, one of our ministers stood and said that he could not conclude a service for Richard without explaining the plan of salvation because no one who was around him for more than five minutes could escape hearing it. The laughter from those assembled at that moment spoke volumes. And when the laughter stilled, they heard again about the love of Jesus Christ that had made such a difference in his life. In death Richard was finally healed, but in life, even though physically broken, he was completely forgiven and delightfully whole.

The Corridor of Life

We can either allow the wounds of life to cripple us, or we can let the Lord Jesus Christ heal our deepest scars and replace our weaknesses with His strength. With Him beside us we, like Richard, can change the script, overcoming seemingly insurmountable obstacles of both nature and nurture to live productive, victorious lives.

In his fine book *Children at Risk*, Dr. James Dobson compares the life of a teenager to a walk down a long corridor. Doors marked "alcohol," "sex," "drugs," "materialism," and so forth line the hallway. From behind every door come the sounds of laughter, fun, music, and beckoning friends. The young person walks down this corridor alone, occasionally hearing his name being called from within. What is there to keep him from opening any door and entering? If parents are not present or have abdicated their authority in a young person's life, there is very little to stop him. Once a door is opened, Dr. Dobson warns, the "monster" lurking within seizes the teenager and too often holds him in a choking grip for the rest of his life. There is great danger in cracking open doors that should remain shut—and in walking the corridor alone!

The corridor, or journey, from childhood to adulthood is lined with doors to opportunities that can easily derail us. Not only are there doors marked "alcohol," "sex," and "drugs" that mask events and experiences that can harm us, there are equally dangerous doors we don't choose, but that seem to open and try to pull us in—doors marked "divorce," "abandonment," "abuse," "conflict," and "loss."

The hallway of Joseph's life was lined with many doors he did not choose. An ineffective father, the early death of his mother, and a blended family that would be considered unusual even by today's loose standards—certainly all these had a profound impact on this young man. His life experience landed him in a pit, in prison, and in exile from his family and his homeland. Few would blame Joseph if he had failed to amount to anything at all.

Instead Joseph navigated the treacherous waters from youth to adulthood with great success. His experience of the true and living God gave him reason to believe and proclaim that no matter what seeming misfortune came his way, God had planned it for good. When we walk with the Living God, the grasping "monsters" from life's hallway have a tough time getting a grip on our lives. The Protector who walked with Joseph will also enable us to overcome all the temptations and barriers we encounter in that daunting corridor. Life's monsters are simply no match for the man or woman who has a vital relationship with the living God.

Joseph's life was good. No, it was great. Not everything in it. Not every instance or circumstance. He had a rather rocky start, and he wondered at times if God had forgotten him, but he didn't mind saying that the end was well worth the journey. He told his children that the secret to his "success" was knowing that God was always with him. If he could have them learn one truth from their father, it would simply be that God's presence in a life is what ultimately sustains. Nothing can defeat the man to whom God is real.

His experience of the true and living God gave him reason to believe and proclaim that no matter what seeming misfortune came his way, God had planned it for good.

More Than Conquerors

Because of his unflagging confidence in the presence of God, Joseph's faith even impressed the pagan Pharaoh of Egypt. "Can we find such a one as this, a man in whom is the Spirit of God?" Pharaoh asked. Joseph was a living illustration of the apostle Paul's declaration in Romans 8:28: "And we know that all things work together for good to those who love God, to those who are the called according to His purpose."

Regardless of what life hands out to us we are not slaves of some deterministic pre-scripted fate. It is not our heredity or environment that definitively shapes us, but our response to them. Sigmund Freud was a psychologist of the determinist school who held that our lives are set on an unalterable course very early on. His young disciple Victor Frankl agreed with Freud until he spent time as a prisoner in a Nazi concentration camp. With every remnant of his physical freedom stripped away, Frankl discovered that there were still a tremendous number of choices available to him in the moments between the atrocities that were committed against him and his fellow prisoners and in their responses to those acts!

Frankl concluded that while he could not control the actions of his captors, he could determine how he would be affected by them. In the midst of a degrading atmosphere that threatened his very life, Victor Frankl became an inspiration to his fellow prisoners and even to some of the Nazi guards. His exercise of the freedom of choice in the face of adversity gave courage and hope to others in the same situation.

A more contemporary example of this mindset is the story of Supreme Court Justice Clarence Thomas. Judge Thomas is viewed by many to be a real-life Horatio Alger who "pulled himself up by his bootstraps" to reach a position of eminence few ever achieve. A *Wall Street Journal* article that appeared shortly after Thomas's nomination in 1991 suggested that his real success story starts as a child who was loved. "The lesson that should not be lost," it said, "is the transcendent one: Clarence Thomas made it in America because he was loved. His mother loved him. And when she could no longer care for him she gave him to her parents to bring up, and they loved him too. He got love, and love gave him pride, and pride gave him confidence that he had a place at the table. This is something we in the age of the family-that-is-not-a-family forget: the raw power of love."

The raw power of love can overcome a bad beginning and carry us through any and every hardship life holds. Clarence Thomas was "kissed and tucked in." So was Joseph. Rusty Welborn was not and neither are countless others. Those of us who are parents have an awesome privilege and responsibility! We can give our children the strong support they so desperately need, and the world can never take it away. We can assure them that they are loved. But for children who do not receive this blessing, there is still hope in the person of Jesus Christ, who can be as real in lives today as God was to Joseph thousands of years ago.

No man, woman, or child is destined to be a victim of heredity or environment. Instead we are to be victors, for "in all these things we are more than conquerors through Him who loved us." The difference between victim and victor is a difference in mindset. The victim focuses on life's injustices, believes he deserves "breaks," waits for someone else to do something for him, has difficulty trusting, and often won't try because he feels all is hopeless. The victor's perspective is radically different. He acknowledges that life is hard, but looks for ways to overcome. He doesn't believe life owes him anything, doesn't wait for others to do what he can do, trusts others even though he knows they may disappoint him, and is willing to try, knowing that success and failure are both facts of life.

We may never have been kissed and tucked in. We may be strangers to the security and nurture of a happy, loving home. But with God's help we can overcome whatever script we've been handed and know that we are loved by the One who is always with us and always working life's circumstances out for our good and His glory.

The Forces That Shape Us

- No human being is created to be a victim. Crises and traumas do not determine the course of our lives. Our responses to those adversities give us our direction.

- When it comes time to answer for the choices we have made in our lives, neither our parents nor our children nor our employers nor our spouses can answer for us. We are individually responsible.
- Scars are inevitable. The wise man doesn't seek to remove them but invites God to use them for His glory and our good.
- Anyone can be whole, regardless of their past. Wholeness is a function of who we are, not where we've been.

Chapter 2

Hi, Dad!
Bye, Dad!

Absentee Fathers

And when Shechem the son of Hamor the Hivite, prince of the country, saw her, he took her and lay with her, and violated her. His soul was strongly attracted to Dinah the daughter of Jacob, and he loved the young woman and spoke kindly to the young woman. So Shechem spoke to his father Hamor, saying, "Get me this young woman as a wife." And Jacob heard that he had defiled Dinah his daughter. Now his sons were with his livestock in the field; so Jacob held his peace until they came.

Genesis 34:2–5

"Where Was George?"

Texas Governor Ann Richards made a name for herself at the 1988 Democratic National Convention with a keynote address that revolved around the rhetorical question, "Where was George?" ("George" was then Vice President George Bush—and he was busy in Washington!) Richards' speech implied that Vice President Bush was not as involved as he should have been in the affairs of the Reagan administration. Her campaign rhetoric was greeted enthusiastically by the Democratic audience, but history reveals that in '88 there were plenty of voters who apparently felt that George was right where he should have been.

The greatest need in our nation today is for godly fathers who are there for their children as leaders and lovers in the home.

Do-nothing Dads

Perceived absenteeism in the political arena is definitely a negative that can cost a candidate votes. The cost of absenteeism in the family can be far more destructive and longer lasting. The greatest need in our nation today is for godly fathers who are there for their children as leaders and lovers in the home.

Joseph's father, Jacob, was the biblical prototype of a modern species that is far from extinct: the do-nothing dad!

Jacob loved his children, but he was not very involved in their day-to-day lives. That fact was clear many times during their years in Shechem but never more powerfully than in his response when his daughter, Dinah, was raped by a Canaanite prince.

Dinah was the daughter of Leah and the prince intended to have her, one way or another, from the moment he first saw her. Perhaps because she was a descendant of Abraham and he was a member of the royal family of King Hamor, he doubted if a legitimate match could be made. Whatever his reasoning, he took her by force and then asked his father, the king, if arrangements could be made for a marriage between them.

You might imagine that Jacob was outraged by this behavior against one of his own children, but you would be wrong. He heard about the defilement of Dinah and decided that in this instance a "wait and see" stance would be best. Her brothers were out in the fields with the livestock at the time, and Jacob did nothing at all until their return. By the time the king of Shechem arrived to bargain with Jacob, the brothers had learned of Dinah's rape and their anger was compounded by their father's lack of concern.

If we could talk to Jacob today about his experience as a father, the interview might go something like this:

"Jacob, what did you do when your daughter Dinah was raped?"

"Well, nothing, but I heard about it, and it really made me mad."

"I see. What about when your sons slaughtered over one thousand people in revenge? Did you do anything then?"

"Oh, that. Nothing. I just thought the sooner we forgot about it the better."

"Jacob, what about when your oldest son Reuben slept with one of your wives? What did you do about that?"

"Well, nothing. I knew that it happened, though . . . and I couldn't believe he didn't know any better. But the embarrassment of a confrontation could have really been unpleasant."

"Jacob, what did you do when you saw the hatred and jealousy that your other ten sons had for Joseph? Didn't you realize your favoritism sowed the seeds of rivalry and division in your home?"

"I guess I didn't realize it would be such a problem. I didn't do anything. I mean, after all boys will be boys."

I remember an older couple with four children from one of my earlier pastorates. They were nominal church-goers who attended often enough for me to know them pretty well but were not really involved in the life of the church. Two of the boys (I'll call them Bill and Bob) were in their late twenties or early thirties. Both still lived in their parents' home in a converted attic room and worked at the same local mill where their father worked. On weekends Bill and Bob followed the practice of so many of the mill workers in this rural town: They would go to one of the local honky tonks, get drunk, and wind up in trouble.

Once in a while they would land in jail, but their father always bailed them out because he was a good, fine, respected man in our community and it just seemed the "fatherly" thing to do. One night I got the phone call I had feared would come eventually. Bill and Bob had been out drinking and, when they returned home, a heated argument erupted. In the brawl that ensued, Bill killed his brother.

I will never forget that funeral service. It was one of the toughest assignments in all my years as a pastor. Bill was brought to the funeral home in police custody, handcuffed to an officer. His mother came to me after the service and asked, "Oh pastor, where did we go wrong?"

That question came a little too late. I could not answer her truthfully at that time, so I simply tried to offer what comfort I could. If I had answered her question honestly, however, I would have pointed to the passivity of that father, whose "goodness" ultimately spelled doom for his sons. The lack of biblical leadership, love, and discipline in their home resulted in devastating loss.

Sometimes more than just a father's leadership is missing in the home, and the results can be tragic. Law enforcement officials in the city of Houston were flabbergasted by a recent case in which a three-year-old girl was taken into custody for selling crack cocaine. As far as they can determine this little girl is the youngest person ever taken into custody in Houston for a felony offense. The child was at home with her mother and three siblings when an undercover officer knocked on the door. She answered the door, asked what the man wanted, and he told her two "dimes," ten dollar rocks of crack cocaine. She returned with the illegal drug and he handed her twenty dollars. The undercover officer stated later that the child was simply doing what her mother had instructed her to do.

*F*atherhood implies a relationship, and a man who is uninvolved in the lives of his children and unaware of their struggles, successes, dreams, and desires is not really a father in the true sense of the word.

When the officer returned with a search warrant, the child's mother and grandmother were gone, and she was taking care of the other children: a two-year-old brother, a one-year-old sister, and a one-month-old sister. Officers later arrested the child's mother (then on parole for a previous drug conviction) and her grandmother. No mention was ever made of the child's father or his whereabouts. Absentee father.

The Love Connection

These two fathers, like far too many of today's dads, had much in common with Jacob: They abdicated their God-given responsibilities as the spiritual leaders of their homes. Jacob was a man who knew God, yet he never applied the knowledge of God and His principles to his role as a father. Being the male biological parent of a child does not make a man a true father, any more than being under a carport would make him a Chevrolet! Fatherhood implies a relationship, and a man who is uninvolved in the lives of his children and unaware of their struggles, successes, dreams, and desires is not really a father in the true sense of the word.

To understand the next part of this story, you must remember that Jacob was not the most honest of men, so his sons did not inherit much respect for honesty. He had deceived his own father, Isaac, and stolen his brother Esau's birthright. And that was not the end of his chicanery. He cheated and he lied, and his sons followed the pattern he had set. So Joseph's brothers accepted King Hamor's offer on the condition that every male of the Canaanite population be circumcised—a condition they amazingly accepted. (You may think that this seems an incredibly high cost for a woman who was already "used," but there was much more at stake. By intermarrying with the sons of Abraham, the Canaanites planned to take control of their livestock and their property, thus increasing their own power.)

On the third day after the Canaanites were circumcised, brothers Simeon and Levi invaded the city and killed every male there with their swords, including the king and his son. They took Dinah from the house of the king, and they looted the city because of what the prince had done to their sister. How did Jacob react? He did nothing. He could hardly condemn them for lying to the Canaanites—he had done as much and more when he was younger.

Too often a father allows the all-consuming quest for fame and fortune to take his time and attention from his family. Even Jacob fell prey to this problem of priorities and found himself climbing the rungs of the ladder of success. When his sons murdered an entire village in revenge for the rape of their sister, he worried more about the monetary ramifications than the moral implications. After all, wiping out an entire village could be bad for business!

His chief concern was not for the mass slaughter of the citizens of the village, but that his sons' actions had made it difficult for him to conduct business. He also feared that the few men left living in the land would band together against him and attack his family. Jacob's sons were incredulous.

They could not believe their father had not defended Dinah's honor. They insisted they had done only what he *should* have done and failed to do.

Our society continues to applaud the successful man more than the family man—but the truth is if you are genuinely a family man, you are a successful man. Frederick Flick was a West German industrialist worth more than $1.5 billion. Prior to his death he controlled some 300 companies and conglomerates. A profile of this highly successful businessman in a national magazine said that he had made all the right moves when it came to accumulating wealth. However every one of his children was a failure. Peter Drucker would have called Flick an undeniable success, and yet according to biblical standards he was a dismal failure. Why? Because he neglected to give his children what they needed from a father: love and leadership. When Flick's wife died, he buried her at 3:00 P.M., went back to the office at 5:00, and never broke stride. However distorted, his priorities were set, and his actions reinforced them at every turn.

*O*ur society continues to applaud the successful man more than the family man—but the truth is if you are genuinely a family man, you are a successful man.

Most fathers would not intentionally shortchange their families or admit that they value their careers over their role as parent. Nevertheless the fact remains that an overwhelming percentage of today's families are without a full-time dad. We have passive fathers in the home because the lion's share of their energy is spent outside of it.

As a boy, my youngest son, Cliff, attended a wonderful camp in North Carolina for several summers. On many occasions he shared with me that some of his fellow campers rarely saw their parents. Many spent the year at boarding school, then attended double sessions of camp during the summer months. This meant they were with their parents only two or three weeks during the year! As a pastor I talk with so many parents who want the church to instill values and to educate their children concerning life. The church can certainly help in these areas and will work with parents in reinforcing life's values, but no church, school, or summer camp can be expected to rear children and successfully guide them through the maze of childhood and adolescence. There is absolutely no substitute for a parent's time in a child's life.

A Man's Family Is Everything

I know a family that has six boys, all fine young men now and away from the nest. People used to tell this father, "Boy, I'd give any amount of money if I could have raised six young men as fine as yours." Wesley Neely had his own thriving lumber business, and it supported the family comfortably. I believe that with his skill and drive he could have been a millionaire, but his business never really skyrocketed like everyone thought it could. The reason? Rather than devote endless time and energy to work, he chose to spend more hours with his sons, especially when they were young.

His choices cost him money, but oh, what he gained! The money Wesley did make wasn't spent on personal hobbies and pleasures. He was much more interested in cultivating his children than accruing capital. True fatherhood is costly—and the currency of parenting is called time.

Today Wesley and Jean Neely's family has grown to include five daughters-in-law and eleven grandchildren. The lumber company is still in business, but Wesley's most valuable investment paid off in the lives of his children. Son Jim is an electrical engineer, is married, and has three children. Jeff is a teacher and basketball coach at Greer High School in Greer, South Carolina. He and his wife are the parents of four children. Paul works as a diesel mechanic with Winn Dixie. He is married, with no children. Bruce followed his dad into the lumber and building construction business. He and his wife have three children. Les, a student of computer electronics, is

"*Quality time*" is a concept invented by the folks who made one-minute management famous.

married with one child. Cam is single and is currently studying auto mechanics. They are still a close family—one that any father would burst with pride to call his own.

He is a wise man who invests in his family. An unfinished letter found by the widow of the late actor Michael Landon shortly after his death from cancer revealed his heart-felt conviction that "a man's family is everything." So many men never understand that until it is too late.

Children Are a Priority

Writer and speaker Jerry B. Jenkins said that one of the commitments he made to his wife, Dianna, early in their marriage was to spend the hours after work and before his children's bedtime with them—no matter what. Even on those evenings when his sons didn't want to play ball or his help with their homework or even to talk with him, he made himself available to them without fail. "Quality time" is a concept invented by the folks who made one-minute management famous. While quality time is important, it cannot compensate for the quantity of time required to rear well-adjusted children. What kids need from their parents (both of them!) is time, time, and more time.

*W*hat kids need from their parents is time, time, and more time.

Perhaps because we are pulled in every direction by the demands of daily life, we cling to the myth that we can plan and schedule the kind of time that will satisfy the needs of our children as we do other "items" and that it will all fit neatly into our already-overloaded agendas. Working parents everywhere breathed a sigh of relief when the concept of "quality time" provided an escape from the guilt caused by parenting on-the-run. What even the hardcore advocates of quality time have discovered, however, is that in actuality such time can rarely be scheduled. It grows out of ordinary everyday events, can cost next-to-nothing, and thrives on spontaneity.

Bathing a pet, planting a shrub, baking cookies, taking a bath, being tucked in at bedtime, or folding the laundry all provide spontaneous opportunities for genuine quality time. The richest moments between parent and child are seldom pre-planned and scheduled on the calendar. *You simply have to be there when they happen.*

Several years ago I was invited to the White House to meet with a few key religious leaders and the President of the United States. Now that was a pretty good offer, wasn't it? It was the first invitation from a president this old country boy from Mississippi had ever received. I'd been out of town during the first part of the week and between flights I called home to check in. When I did, I learned that my son Ben's basketball game originally scheduled for mid-week had been re-scheduled for the end of the week—and I'd missed one game already!

The question was one of simple priority: "What's the most important thing to me?" Since the government had been running pretty well without me for a number of years, I called the White House and said, "Ed Young won't be coming." (They recovered from this news beautifully.) Instead I went to the game and had the fun of seeing my son shoot the winning basket. I have to confess that deciding between the White House and the school gym was not too tough. My wife and my boys are my highest priority.

Ancient Advice for Modern Dads

Without a personal, passionate, devoted relationship to the Lord Jesus Christ, it is difficult for any man to be the kind of father whose children will one day call him "blessed."

Jacob did not have the kind of resources we have today on the subject of learning to be an effective father. After all, there were not many parenting seminars taught in West Canaan in his day! And yet in the pages of Deuteronomy, one of the books of the Pentateuch, right in the middle of Jewish law we discover these timeless words of wisdom:

You shall love the LORD your God with all your heart, with all your soul, and with all your strength. And these words which I command you today shall be in your heart. You shall teach them diligently to your children, and shall talk of them when you sit in your house, when you walk by the way, when you lie down, and when you rise up. You shall bind them as a sign on your hand, and they shall be as frontlets between your eyes. You shall write them on the doorposts of your house and on your gates.

Deuteronomy 6:5–9

This passage speaks of two principles that are critical to men who would be effective fathers: one, a personal loving devotion to God Himself, and two, something I call "saturation leadership." Without a personal, passionate, devoted relationship to the Lord Jesus Christ, it is difficult for any man to be the kind of father whose children will one day call him "blessed." God's strength and guidance are essential because the job is enormous.

The rest of this passage establishes the second principle, the idea of a continual and multi-faceted approach to teaching your children what really matters in life. This approach speaks of consistency. It speaks of personal example. It requires time, and it means that every word heard or every action observed bears a solid witness to our children that our agenda and God's agenda are one and the same. Most importantly, in time it becomes as natural as breathing. The method is simply teach/talk/write/bind. In everything we do, we must demonstrate that God comes first. We need to live out the principles of God's Word in a transparent and honest way before our children. This scripture says we are to wear God's commands on our foreheads, and the Jews of the Old Testament literally did just that. They wore headbands that contained the law as a reminder of their covenant with God in much the same way that a wedding band today reminds us of our covenants with our mates. The idea is simply to keep our commitment before us at all times.

Big Mouth/ Big Ear

A teenager was asked what he pictured when he thought of his father. His response was almost instantaneous: "a big mouth." When asked what he would like to see, he was equally as quick to reply: "a big ear." Perhaps the most important instruction in Moses' words is to talk to our children. Communication is a two-way exchange! Jacob may have observed his sons, but it doesn't appear that he either talked to them much or knew the condition of their hearts. In fact, he seemed more interested in commerce than communication.

Our three sons are as different as they can be, but Jo Beth and I have made communicating with them one of our highest priorities. Our oldest, Ed, would talk anytime. With him everything was out in the open—no hidden agendas, no secrets, just a constant flow of words and information. Ben, our middle son, was more reticent. He would hold back until he was ready to talk, but then he'd let go—and often it was at times we'd just as soon be asleep, like midnight on a Saturday night! Our youngest son, Cliff, thank goodness, is a happy blend of both. With all three, when they were ready to talk, we tried our best to be ready to listen.

Too many fathers never learn to communicate with their children, and the silence that begins in childhood remains unbroken. Playwright Moss Hart capsulized this kind of heartbreaking estrangement in his autobiography when he described a walk with his father on Christmas Eve the year he was ten. The Harts were quite poor, but Moss's father took him down to 149th Street and Westchester in New York City that night, past countless toy vendors' pushcarts. Moss strolled with his father past the carts, eyeing chemistry sets and printing presses with obvious longing.

"I looked up and saw we were nearing the end of the line. Only two or three more pushcarts remained. My father looked up, too, and I heard him jingle some coins in his pocket. In a flash I knew it all. He'd gotten together about seventy-five cents to buy me a Christmas present, and he hadn't dared say so in case there was nothing to be had for so small a sum.

"As I looked up at him I saw a look of despair and disappointment in his eyes that brought me closer to him than I had ever been in my life. I wanted to throw my arms around him and say 'It doesn't matter . . . I understand . . . This is better than a chemistry set or a printing press . . . I love you.' But instead we stood shivering beside each other for a moment—then turned silently back home. I don't know why the words remained choked up within me. I didn't even take his hand on the way home, nor did he take mine. *We were not on that basis.*"[1]

We expect our children to speak our language and to operate on our timetables. Instead, when our children are ready to speak, we must be ready to listen and we must learn to speak their language. Contrast Moss Hart's story of his father with the stories we know of Jesus, a man who not only understood the language of children but loved to communicate with them.

The Gospel of Mark records an occasion where children approached Jesus and were shooed away by His disciples. Those old disciples believed that their Master had more important things to do than babysit. But do you remember how Jesus responded? He reprimanded them and then personally invited the children into his arms so that He could hold and bless them, saying, "Let the little children come to Me, and do not forbid them."

When our children are ready to speak, we must be ready to listen and we must learn to speak their language.

Now Jesus was a busy man. His agenda was ambitious to say the least! But His actions said that nothing in His schedule was more important to Him than those children—not preaching, not teaching, and not healing the sick. He gave children His first priority.

When our children are ready to speak, we must be ready to listen and we must learn to speak their language.

Father Knows Best

Proverbs 22:6 instructs parents to "Train up a child in the way he should go, and when he is old he will not depart from it." Far from being an instruction to fathers to impose their own dogmatic constraints on their children, this verse is a plea for fathers to study their children to determine their unique "bent," and guide them in that way.

The father who truly knows best is the father who knows his children—their gifts, their desires, their abilities, and their natural leanings. The wise father leads his child, not in the way he would choose, but as the child is "bent" by God Himself! To do this we must become students of our children—a practice that is entertaining, informative, and essential to effective parenting. (There are times, too, when we see ourselves in our children, and the revelation can be a painful one!)

When Parental Love Goes Wrong

If there is anything sadder than a father who abandons his responsibility for his children, it is the one who abuses them. Recently our local paper ran two equally shocking stories of parental abuse—one contemporary and one chronicling events that occurred decades ago.

In one, an eight-year-old child testified against her parents in a bond hearing after they were charged with the beating and starving death of the girl's five-year-old sister. The father and mother, an Indiana heart surgeon and a former nurse, were accused by their daughter of inflicting punishments that ranged from regular beatings to being forced to drink milk laced with black pepper. Medical testimony at the hearing indicated that the younger daughter may have choked to death as a result of this last "punishment." Testimony from one of the older daughter's psychotherapists revealed that the parents not only injected themselves with painkilling drugs, they gave them to their daughters as well. (The parents were held without bail.)

The second story involved Marilyn Van Derber Atler, Miss America of 1957, who recently revealed that as a child she was sexually abused by her millionaire father. Her statement was both chilling and sad: "A list of all my accomplishments—times one hundred—pales before the only real accomplishment of my life, said in only three words: I survived incest."

Atler's father was the late Francis Van Derber, millionaire businessman, socialite, philanthropist, and pillar of the community. Atler's confession came as she, her husband of twenty-three years, and her mother sought to emphasize the work of a survivor program at the Kempe Center in Denver for adults who were sexually abused as children.

Atler said her father's abuse continued from the time she was five until she was eighteen but that she did not fully recognize what had happened to her until she was twenty-five. She concluded the interview by stating, "As difficult as this is for most people to understand . . . I loved my father. It is innocent children and mute adults that I hope to set free. If I cannot speak the truth with my father dead, how, dear God, can we expect a child to speak?"

*F*or every person who lives with the memory of an earthly father who failed, there is the promise of a heavenly Father who will not—who cannot fail.

I hope these examples are as foreign and shocking to you as they are to me, but I know that for some reading this book they will not be. If you had no father, an absent father, or an abusive one, you know far better than I the effects these situations can have well into adulthood. You can choose to be bound to the past, or you can look at it honestly and let God set you free from its devastating web of pain. It will be difficult. Making the choice to overcome your hurt may be the easiest part of the process. But for every person who lives with the memory of an earthly father who failed, there is the promise of a heavenly Father who will not—who cannot fail.

Hi, Dad! Bye, Dad!

Every summer our church takes its high school and junior high students on a week-long beach retreat. Last summer about 700 kids "invaded" Panama Beach, Florida, for this time of fun and spiritual encouragement. In order to attend the retreat, each student must fill out a rather detailed application that helps us see where they are in their spiritual development and alerts us to any problems they may be facing with their friends or families.

One of the questions on last year's application was "If you were to write a book about your family, what would the title of that book be?" One of our junior high students said that his book would be called *Hi, Dad! Bye, Dad!* I believe that title says volumes about this young man's family and about the families of many today, both inside and outside the church.

If your personal story is one of parental neglect or disappointment or abuse, I hope you will begin today to allow the Father who is love to become the loving father you never had. He is the one who will always say "hi" and never say "bye." He will not fail, and He will be there for His children—for you.

Those of us who are fathers face a tremendous challenge. General Motors can recall cars, but it is impossible for us to recall the character-building years of our children. When they are gone, they are gone. Jacob could not go back, neither can we. He would suffer for the rest of his life from the mistakes he made in raising his sons—and they suffered too. Fathering is a lifetime job. Let's not miss a single opportunity to "punch in" as a real dad.

A Father's Responsibilities

- The most significant gift any father can give his children is his time. Nothing is more valuable.

- Our children need to know that they have top priority with us—ahead of our jobs, our social lives, and our hobbies.
- Because we teach best by example, we need to be what we are shaping our children to become.
- When our children are ready to talk we must be ready to listen—and we must learn to communicate in their unique language.
- Nothing prepares a man for fatherhood better than a personal, passionate, devoted relationship with our Heavenly Father through Jesus Christ.
- A family man is a successful man, regardless of the world's definition of success.

Chapter 3

Life in the Blender

Divorce/Blended Families

Now the sons of Jacob were twelve: the sons of Leah were Reuben, Jacob's firstborn, and Simeon, Levi, Judah, Issachar, and Zebulun; the sons of Rachel were Joseph and Benjamin; the sons of Bilhah, Rachel's maidservant, were Dan and Naphtali; and the sons of Zilpah, Leah's maidservant, were Gad and Asher.

Genesis 35:22–26

Life in the Blender

The word *family* once conjured similar images for most people. We thought of Thanksgiving dinners, Christmas mornings, birthdays, tender moments, and sticking together through thick and thin. Today, however, other thoughts also come to mind—thoughts of weekends at Dad's, sharing rooms with step-brothers and step-sisters, and holidays spent juggling schedules so each parent can share a portion of the time with their children.

Today only 27 percent of American families fit the traditional model of two parents married "till death do us part," living with the children they both share. In fact this scenario is now so rare that many refer to it as the "mythical family"—at best an endangered species, and at worst an irrelevant, outdated relic.

What has happened to the family in the last twenty-five years? To answer this question, we need to take a long, hard look at the trauma of divorce.

The Impact of Divorce

Our relational vocabulary has expanded to include terms like *binuclear family* and *no-fault divorce* as we attempt to explain the changes that have taken place in the family over the last quarter of a century. In the 1960s, 37 percent of all first-time marriages in America ended in divorce.

Seventy-nine percent of those who divorced remarried—and 44 percent of those second marriages also ended in divorce. During the 1970s and 1980s the statistics grew even worse, with one of every two marriages ending in divorce. In forty-one American jurisdictions today, a spouse can terminate a marriage without the partner's consent and without proving fault.

*W*e are just beginning to understand the effects of divorce on individuals, families, and society as a whole.

We are just beginning to understand the effects of divorce on individuals, families, and society as a whole. One of every four children born in the 1980s will live in a step-family by age eighteen. In 90 percent of the divorces involving children, mothers retain sole custody, and even in joint custody situations, children spend only about 30 percent of their time with their fathers. Fifty-two percent of all divorced women have custody of minor children, and sadly, these children are the primary and most vulnerable victims of broken marriages.

The decline of the traditional family is changing the very landscape of childhood. Consider these sobering statistics:

- Twenty percent of American children grow up in poverty—a 21 percent increase since 1970.
- There are 330,000 homeless children in our nation today.
- The suicide rate among children and adolescents has tripled in the last thirty years.
- The drop-out rate among teenagers is rising—27 percent currently drop out of high school.
- The instance of child abuse nationwide has quadrupled since 1975.
- In 1971, 6,500 teenagers were hospitalized in private psychiatric facilities in the U.S. By 1989 the number had reached almost 200,000.
- The average American teenager has spent the equivalent of an entire work year watching *television commercials alone* by age eighteen.

Children of Divorce

Psychologist Judy Wallerstein's 1989 report on the long-term effects of divorce on families *(Second Chances: Men, Women and Children a Decade After Divorce)* confirmed what many have feared for some time: The effects of divorce on children are often traumatic and long-lasting. While many parents assume that their relief or happiness at the end of a difficult marriage will ultimately mean better lives for their children, this is not necessarily true.

Of the 131 children in Wallerstein's study, only 10 percent reported feeling relief at their parents' divorce. Almost half the children she followed for ten or more years entered adulthood as "worried, under-achieving, self-deprecating and sometimes angry young men and women." A wide variety of long-term effects are evident in the children of divorce. As they approach adulthood, many of these children are unable to commit to love relationships of their own and experience clinical depression, guilt, and protracted grief.

In divorce children lose their family structure, the very thing that they depend on to support their development from childhood, through adolescence, and into adulthood.

In divorce children lose their family structure, the very thing that they depend on to support their development from childhood, through adolescence, and into adulthood. The loss can be confusing and emotionally crippling.

One small child of divorced parents expressed anxiety in the afternoons when he became confused about which parent would pick him up from preschool on which days. His mother's solution, while helpful, paints a sad picture of a fragmented family: She began giving him two lunchboxes—a red one for "Daddy Days" and a green one for "Mommy Days."

Navigating the swirling waters of divorce is a difficult task. It is hard enough for two people who are no longer husband and wife to continue to parent their children as an effective team. But when either ex-spouse remarries, the arrangement becomes even more complex. Now step-brothers, step-sisters, a new set of grandparents, and a step-parent are added to an already awkward family equation. If a remarried parent has other children with the new spouse, the family can seemingly become a "cast of thousands."

*U*nlike the Bradys, most blended families do not exist in a "relational vacuum."

Yours, Mine, and Ours

Some years ago a situation comedy called *The Brady Bunch* appeared on television. You may remember the Bradys as they were described in the show's catchy theme song: an eligible bachelor named Mike who was raising three sons on his own, and a lovely lady named Carol who was doing the same with her three daughters. (I'll bet you're humming along already.) Their blended family (Marsha, Jan, Cindy, Greg, Peter, Bobby, and Alice, the maid) had an occasional spat, but for the most part was an idyllic example of successful, harmonious domesticity.

There was only one thing wrong with the Bradys—their story was totally unrealistic! The show, while it was entertaining, implied that all it takes to maintain a blended family is organization, and that any problem, no matter how serious, can be solved in thirty minutes or less. I've never known six children from the *same* parents to get along as well as these six from different families appeared to!

Unlike the Bradys, most blended families do not exist in a "relational vacuum." There are grandparents. There are in-laws. There are ex-husbands and ex-wives. (And there's seldom a maid!) In *The Brady Bunch*, forming one loving family from two separate homes was a piece of cake, but in real life, it's a tremendous challenge.

For a more realistic picture of some of the obstacles and challenges a blended family might encounter, we need look only as far as "Jacob's Bunch" in the pages of Genesis. The patriarch Jacob had twelve sons and four wives, two of whom were sisters.

It happened this way. Joseph's grandfather, Laban, had two daughters—Rachel, the younger, and Leah, the older. Jacob loved Rachel so much that he offered to serve Laban seven years for the right to be her husband. At the end of the seven years, a wedding took place. And when Jacob lifted his bride's veil, she wasn't Rachel, but her homelier sister, Leah. When he confronted his dishonest father-in-law, Laban said it was not the practice of his people to marry the younger daughter before the elder. Then he promised that in a week's time, he would give Jacob his daughter Rachel as well (for a price, of course: seven additional years of service to Laban). So Jacob began his life as a husband with the two sisters as his wives.

The competition, I am sure, was fierce. Although Jacob loved Rachel more than Leah, God opened Leah's womb, and she began to bear him children. She named the first son Reuben, and she believed that his birth would win her Jacob's love. She conceived again and bore a second son, whom she named Simeon. Her third son was Levi. With the birth of each one Leah hoped that Jacob would grow more attached to her, for Rachel had not yet borne him a child. After the birth of a fourth son, Judah, Leah stopped bearing children.

Rachel's heart was sick and she longed for children. Her failure to have them as easily as her sister was one of the few things she and Jacob fought about. Finally Rachel sent her maid Bilhah to Jacob, and she bore him a son named Dan. Rachel considered him her own, but Bilhah did not. Bilhah conceived again and bore yet another son whom she named Naphtali. While Leah had borne no more children, not wanting to be outdone by Rachel's handmaid, she gave her own maid, Zilpah, to Jacob as a fourth wife. Zilpah had two sons; Gad and Asher were their names.

A petty quarrel between Rachel and Leah caused Jacob to lie again with Leah, and to their surprise she conceived yet again. This child, another son, was named Issachar. The sixth and last son Leah gave to Jacob was called Zebulun, and afterward she bore him a daughter, Dinah.

It was after Dinah's birth that God remembered Rachel's plight and opened her womb. Joseph was the first son born to Jacob and Rachel. This longing granted, the greatest desire of Rachel's heart was for another son. That son, Benjamin, was born as they were traveling to Bethlehem and Rachel died after his birth. She was buried on the way, and Jacob set a pillar over her grave.

That was Joseph's family: his father, Jacob, a mother who died when he was young, ten half-brothers, one half-sister, and a younger brother, Benjamin. They lived together in adjoining tents like a wandering tribe, and the strain was sometimes unbearable. Competition between wives and children was relentless. For his part, Jacob seemed unaffected by it all. But his family felt the tension of his choices every day of their lives.

Can't you imagine the animosity between the siblings in Jacob's household? "My mother's better than your mother," or "Dad loves me and my brothers best," or even more ridiculous, "Our tent is bigger than your tent." Just their living situation fostered unbelievable rivalry. Frequently this continual strife resulted in violence, both inside the family and outside it.

> *F*or his part, Jacob seemed unaffected by it all. But his family felt the tension of his choices every day of their lives.

The War No One Wins

It has been said that children become the reluctant bullets in the war of divorce. They provide both ex-spouses with ideal weapons in the ongoing game of vengeance since they are trusting, eager to please, and easily manipulated. In a recent *People* magazine feature on children of divorce, a young man in California expressed the pain of his parents' custody arrangement this way: "The divorce was like the marriage. They just split everything down the middle, including me." In addition to being used as weapons in their parents' battles, the young are exposed to increasing violence *outside* the home as well. Researchers say this chaos also results from a breakdown in the traditional nuclear family.

Growing up with only one parent's time, attention, discipline, and love is a handicap that is not easily overcome. The National Association of Elementary School Principals conducted a major study of children from single-parent families. Their findings were quite significant. Thirty percent of two-parent elementary students were considered high achievers, as opposed to 17 percent of single-parent households. Single-parent students were also more likely to be absent, late, truant, and subject to disciplinary action than were students from two-parent households. Single-parent children were also twice as likely to drop out of school altogether. Seventy percent of the juveniles in state reform institutions grew up in single-parent or no-parent families.

When a Washington, D.C. city official visited an eighth grade class for gifted children in that city in 1987, he asked the students about their exposure to violent crime. Fourteen of nineteen students said they personally knew someone who had been murdered. In the city of Detroit at about the same time, 102 children aged sixteen or younger were shot, most of them by other children. In the city of Houston, reports of violence by school-aged children are common. Many schools, especially in large metropolitan districts, have established standard security precautions just so students can attend class with some degree of safety ensured by school administrators.

What can we learn from these alarming trends? That there is no adequate substitute for the intact family unit. Nothing that educators, the government,

"The divorce was like the marriage. They just split everything down the middle, including me."

*A*s much as we'd like to believe in the Brady Bunch, real-life blended families today bear a much stronger resemblance to Jacob's Bunch.

psychologists, or sociologists can offer us successfully replaces a strong, supportive family in the life of a child. As much as we'd like to believe in the Brady Bunch, real-life blended families today bear a much stronger resemblance to Jacob's Bunch. Jealousy, conflict, and anger too often evolve into dysfunctional situations, and sometimes, as in the case of Jacob's sons, acts of violence.

While raising a child alone is a formidable challenge, it is by no means a new one. The first single parent I know of is found in the Bible in the book of Genesis. Her name was Hagar and she was the maidservant of Sarah, wife of Abraham. God had promised Abraham and Sarah a whole nation of descendants, but they were very old and were childless. Sarah (apparently thinking that God needed a little help to keep His promise) sent her husband in to lie with Hagar so that a child would be conceived that Abraham and Sarah could raise as their own. The child of Abraham and Hagar was named Ishmael, and he and his mother lived with Abraham and Sarah until he was a young teenager.

Then when Abraham was one hundred years old, his son Isaac was born to Sarah, and that's when the trouble started. She quickly demanded that Hagar and Ishmael be banished. So Abraham sent this single mother and her young son away to the wilderness with a skin of water and a loaf of bread. When they had wandered far and were near starvation, Hagar left Ishmael crying under a bush and sat down opposite him, crying out to God. Then the Bible tells us that an amazing thing happened:

> And God heard the voice of the lad. Then the angel
> of God called to Hagar out of heaven, and said to
> her, "What ails you, Hagar? Fear not, for God has
> heard the voice of the lad where he is. Arise, lift up

the lad and hold him with your hand, for I will
make him a great nation." Then God opened her
eyes, and she saw a well of water. And she went and
filled the skin with water, and gave the lad a drink.
So God was with the lad; and he grew and dwelt in
the wilderness, and became an archer.

Genesis 21:17–20

Single parents, God is with your children. Psalm 68:5–6 contains a promise that is particularly comforting to a mother who is raising her children alone. It says that God is the father of the fatherless, and that He sets the lonely in families.

It Would Take Too Long and Hurt Too Much

While some of the statistics I've cited on blended families paint a bleak picture, it is by no means impossible to overcome the odds and raise up godly children in spite of a broken home. Young Joseph is our biblical example of this truth. In my years as a pastor I've seen other examples as well. One family in particular stands out in my memory. The Richards separated when their son Mac was twelve and twins Pattrick and Gil were ten.

Mac remembers a conversation with his parents prior to their divorce in which he shared his concern for a young classmate whose mom and dad were separating. They were driving in the car as they talked, and he recalls his dad turning around and saying, "Well, son, that's something you'll never have to worry about—that's not the way your mother and I think."

Five years later, on a sunny afternoon in mid-September, this young family came apart. The Houston Oilers were playing the Cleveland Browns in a football game that had gone into overtime. The boys were sitting in front of the television, wrapped up in the excitement of Sunday afternoon football, when their parents came out of their bedroom and their dad turned off the game, saying, "Fellas, we need to talk."

Mac says he vividly recalls that although the word *divorce* was never spoken, he understood that it was a certainty. His father explained that he had some problems to work through and had to do that by himself. He told his sons he still loved them and that his leaving was not their fault. Then he left with a bag of clothes, a Bible, and a promise that he would see them again in a month, leaving his shell-shocked wife and sons in tears.

Are you wondering if this was a church-going family? They were. Tom was a deacon and Sunday school teacher. They were faithful attenders. Mac went to see his dad three months later and asked him if the God he'd always talked to his sons about wasn't able to make whatever went wrong, right. His father confessed that he believed God could but that it would take too long and hurt too much. He just refused to try.

As is often the case after a divorce, the mother became the primary means of support and nurture for her children. Tom remarried, had another child with his new wife, and was only marginally involved in the lives of his sons from that point on. Over the years I have watched these three boys grow into fine young men. Mac is attending seminary and serving on a church staff in Dallas. Patrick and Gil are currently college students. All three have been active leaders in the youth ministry of our church. Linda taught school when the boys were younger and now serves on our church staff.

How did this family fractured by divorce beat the odds? One of the boys let the secret slip as he gave his personal testimony to a group of our high school kids last year. He said the strongest memory of his childhood years was seeing his mother night after night by her bed, kneeling in prayer. A godly mother and the personal relationship each one of these young men cultivated in the Lord Jesus Christ made the difference.

Just this summer I had the opportunity to celebrate the against-the-odds survival of this family again when Mac married one of my own nieces. As I watched Patrick and Gil escort their mother into the church and saw Mac waiting expectantly at the altar for his bride, I was overwhelmed at the goodness and sufficiency of the God who became a father to these young men. And I was reminded that, no matter what the circumstances, there is hope for a family broken by divorce.

Making It Work

If you are a member of a blended or single-parent family today, let me encourage you and assure you that there is hope! Here are some practical guidelines that can ease the way for the "yours, mine, and ours" family:

Guidelines for Parents

- *Present a unified front of discipline to your children.* If you and your ex-spouse are sharing child-rearing responsibilities, strive to reach agreement between you on how you will establish and enforce discipline. Never allow your children to play one parent against the other. If you are parenting alone, make sure your children know that your word is no less definitive because it is singular. Be consistent in the way you administer discipline to each child.
- *Do all within your power to enhance your children's relationship with your former spouse.* As much as is humanly possible, separate the problems of your former marital relationship from

your ongoing roles as parents. There is nothing to gain by telling your children how wrong their other parent is. It is not essential that you like each other. It is important that you cooperate as much as possible for the sake of your children. It is a sad, sad sight to see parents compete for the love of their children. No one wins.

- *Respect routines.* Structure is important to a child. Work together to establish new routines as a blended family. Give children time to adapt to change, and above all, respect the routines they had in their previous family arrangement. Do your best to incorporate existing traditions and routines into your new structure. One of the saddest sights to me now is an airport terminal over the holidays or when school is out. There are so many "unaccompanied minors" being shuffled around this nation to spend Christmas with this parent, summer vacation with that parent, spring break with grandparents, and on and on. It breaks my heart to see it! Be sensitive to these times and work to make them as painless as possible. Every time the holiday shuffle takes place, the children are reminded all over again that theirs is not a "normal" family.

- *Make knowing your children and supporting them your highest priority.* Be involved in their lives. Know their dreams. Support their interests. When there is a game, a play, a recital, give them the assurance that you want to, and will, be there to cheer them on. Children need to know that they are more important to their parents than work, hobbies, or a social calendar could ever be.

- *Teach your children to depend on God.* Only as they see you and me rely upon the Father will they begin to understand His utter reliability and faithfulness.

Guidelines for Children

- *Don't blame yourself for your parents' divorce.* As a child you viewed yourself as the center of all that happened around you. Although this self-centered viewpoint is common in children, it can distort the realities of divorce. Resist the urge to parent your parents and choose instead to live out your childhood. You are not the cause of your parents' failed marriage, and you cannot "save" or hold together a marriage covenant that has no other support. You are not the problem, and you cannot solve the problem, no matter how good you are or how hard you try.

- *Realize that divorce is wrong, but it is not unredeemable.* Divorce is never God's best for a man or a woman, but the fact that one or both of your parents chose divorce does not sentence you to a second-best kind of life. You belong to God. Divorce is a kind of "crucible," and through it you can be made strong. He will not abandon you because your parents' marriage did not survive.
- *Refuse to be an informer for either of your parents.* It is not your job to carry information from one parent to another or to inform one parent of what the other parent is doing. They are adults, and they are capable of communicating with each other as they choose without your intervention. Love both of your parents unreservedly and refuse to fight one parent's battles against the other. Even if you believe one was right and the other wrong, do not fall into the trap of rewarding the innocent parent with your love and punishing the guilty parent by withholding it.
- *Accept your parents' choices of other mates if remarriage occurs.* You can gain nothing by refusing to acknowledge a new step-father or step-mother. No, a step-parent is not your mother or father. But he or she has been chosen by your mother or father to share his or her life, and your hostility toward that choice will only further fragment your family. If you can, see yourself as God's missionary in this place of re-adjustment and change and seek to make Him known in the midst of it. You can be sure that this attitude will please your Heavenly Father and will do more to right the situation than your negative response.
- *Honor your parents, period.* As a child this is your instruction from God, and it is what He requires of you, regardless of their worth

or behavior. There was an old military maxim that says, "If you can't salute the man, salute the bars." If you cannot condone your parents' actions or respect them as people, you can acknowledge that God has placed them in authority over you, and for that reason alone they deserve your honor.

If you are single, you may be thinking that nothing I have said thus far is applicable to your situation, but I've saved my last word on divorce, remarriage, and the family just for you. You (and the choices you make) will determine the state of your home and family in the future.

If you are considering marriage, be certain that the individual you plan to marry not only professes to be a Christian, but desires and intends to be obedient to the scripture in this all-important area of life. God cannot honor relationships where two people are unequally yoked. You'll go a long way toward beating the odds by marrying someone who is spiritually mature and committed to a "till death do us part" kind of union. Choose wisely. The future of your family depends on it.

Beating the Broken Home

- Divorce is rarely a solution—and always a complication.
- When marriages fail, our children pay a higher price than anyone.
- Nothing can replace the security of a stable home in the life of a child.
- A blended family will have adjustment problems, and they cannot always be solved immediately. It takes time and commitment to make one family out of two.
- God promises the single parent that He is a father to the fatherless and will set the lonely in families.
- Nothing can better equip us to survive a broken family than a personal relationship with Jesus Christ.

Chapter 4

Discipline

Dos and Don'ts

Now Israel loved Joseph more than all his children, because he was the son of his old age. Also he made him a tunic of many colors. But when his brothers saw that their father loved him more than all his brothers, they hated him and could not speak peaceably to him.

Genesis 37:3–4

Discipline: Dos and Don'ts

Dr. James Dobson tells one of my favorite stories about the effects of poor parenting choices on the life of a child. The young fellow in this story was a patient of California pediatrician Dr. William Slonecker, and his name was Robert. When Robert was scheduled for a visit to the doctor's office, the news would spread like wildfire: "Batten down the hatches! *Robert* is coming!"

Nurses steeled themselves in preparation for this ten-year-old undisciplined terror who tore magazines out of their holders, threw trash all over the waiting room, and wreaked havoc throughout the clinic. Each time his mother would simply shake her head and say, "Oh, Robert. Oh, Robert." If the office staff corrected him in any way, he would bite, kick, and scream his way back to his seat. When his visit with the doctor was over, Robert would come out of the examining room wailing and crying—a practice that always terrified the other children waiting their turn!

During one of his examinations, Dr. Slonecker noticed that Robert had a few cavities, an observation that presented the doctor with a real professional dilemma. He needed to refer Robert to a dentist but hated to inflict him on a good friend or associate. Finally one dentist who had an unusual rapport with children came to mind, so he rather reluctantly made the referral.

Robert saw his trip to the dentist as a new and exciting challenge in an ongoing battle of wills. As he was ushered into the examining room, he announced to the dentist that he had no intention of getting into the chair.

*T*here is no child alive who will not, at one time or other, try to manipulate his parents.

"Now, Robert," the old dentist replied, "I'm not going to force you, but I want you to climb up into the chair." Robert bowed his little head and screamed his refusal. The dentist patiently explained that Robert must sit in the chair so his teeth could be fixed. Robert refused once again—loudly. As the dentist moved toward him, Robert played what he was certain was the trump card: "If you come over here and try to make me, I'll take off all my clothes." Calmly, the wise old dentist said, "Fine, son, you go right ahead."

Robert removed his shoes and shirt and stood defiantly. The doctor did not back down. Robert continued removing his clothing until he stood there just as naked as the day he was born. "Now Robert," said the dentist, "you climb on up yourself." And a naked (and surprised) ten-year-old terror climbed up into the chair and sat motionless as his teeth were filled. No crying. No screaming. No hitting or slapping.

When the dentist was finished, Robert climbed down and asked for his clothes. "No, son," the good doctor replied, "I'm going to keep your clothes overnight. Tell your mother she can come by tomorrow to pick them up." So a bested Robert walked out into the waiting room . . . naked. His mother took him by the hand, led him down the hall, and out into the parking lot to their car.

The next morning Robert's mother returned to the office for her son's clothes and asked to speak to the conquering dentist. When he came out she said, "Doctor, I want to thank you for what you did to Robert yesterday. Since he was very young he has threatened us with a host of things if he did not get his way. We never called his bluff. But since you did, he has been a different child!"

There is no child alive who will not, at one time or other, try to manipulate his parents. Children are born with a bent to disobedience, and they will attempt a variety of creative schemes in order to get their way (just like adults do!). We saw in the preceding chapter that Jacob was a passive father who abdicated much of his responsibility as a parent. When this happens children, not their parents, become the controlling influence in the home, often with devastating results.

Jacob fell prey to some of parenthood's most common traps. He was absent as the authority figure in his own home. He allowed himself to show favoritism to one child over the others.

He overlooked the rivalry between his children that his own poor choices fostered. And perhaps most important, he failed to exercise the discipline that might have righted these other mistakes and allowed his children to grow comfortably and securely into productive adults.

How does a father establish leadership? What does a father who is effective in this area look like? Why did Jacob not fit the mold? Maybe the media can help us. Remember Dagwood Bumstead? Dagwood was the cartoon dad who was propped up by his wife and children. He meant well, but he was inept, crazy, mistake-prone, and ineffective. Dagwood was funny, but he was not a good model of parental leadership.

How about Archie Bunker? Archie was the prototypical bigot who ran the Bunker household with an iron fist. He was prejudiced, opinionated, and argumentative. Confident of his rightness and assured in his intellect, he browbeat his daughter, Gloria, and wife, Edith, who rarely questioned his authority. Archie was in charge, but he was not effective.

John Walton was a dad I liked a lot. John was hard-working, fair, loyal, and loving as a father. He knew his children. He had wisdom, foresight, and a sense of timing when it came to parenting. As TV dads go, Mr. Walton was not a bad example.

A newer media father was embodied by Bill Cosby's Cliff Huxtable. Cliff was a fun-loving obstetrician with an attorney wife and a mixed bag of kids, each one unique. While he made value judgments I did not always agree with as a Christian, Cliff communicated with his children. He talked to them, knew their interests and activities, and was an active participant in their lives.

Of course, each of these fathers is fictional, the product of a writer's imagination, but they possess characteristics of real dads, and that's why we can relate so easily to them.

I can recall from my growing-up years fathers who embodied other stereotypes. Maybe you remember them too. The one I'll call "the drill sergeant" gave orders. He was always gone for some personal reason. Golf. Business meetings. Poker games. But when he was there, he was on top of everything. He had that "I'm in charge here" mentality, and he was the undisputed leader of his home.

Then there was "the dictator." He was at home all of the time, and when he was there, his family waited on him hand and foot. He had plenty of things for everyone to do—so many, in fact, that they were relieved when he went to work. When he came home they would hide from him!

Finally, there was "the passive father." You know the one. The last decision he made was at the marriage altar. Either his wife runs the home or no one does. She is the commandant, and he simply walks around on eggshells all the time. Some of the fathers who fit these types would tell you that they *could* have been effective; they just weren't lucky. All they needed was a more understanding wife, better children, or a different job. I don't buy that for a second, and neither should you. Being an effective father has nothing to do with luck, and it has everything to do with leadership. Had Jacob been a stronger leader, many of the problems between his children could have been alleviated or avoided entirely.

Sibling Rivalry

Hands down, Joseph was his father's favorite son. He knew it and so did his brothers. He was the son of the woman Jacob chose before any other, and he was the son of Jacob's old age. His parents prayed and waited many years for Joseph.

Jacob, of all people, should have recognized the heartbreak this could cause. He had been the favorite of his mother, Rebekah, while his brother,

Esau, was the red-haired apple of Isaac's eye. And years later, he repeated the same scenario in his own home. Jacob showed his favor for Joseph by giving him a coat of many colors. It would have been an ankle-length garment cinched at the waist and probably was crafted and sewn with elaborate embroidery by Jacob himself. The coat was like those worn by royalty, and it identified young Joseph as the heir to his father's fortune. It was opulent, luxurious, and by no means did it qualify as "working gear." This visible token of affection was the straw that broke the brothers' backs!

What it bred in his brothers was jealousy—and it "cloaked" Joseph in an environment of bitter jealousy because of the brothers' reaction to this lavish gift. If Jacob had exercised wisdom in dealing with his children, he could have done much to avoid the conflicts that developed between them. Had Joseph been older and a little more mature when this gift was given, he might have handled his father's obvious favoritism more responsibly. Unfortunately this kind of destructive favoritism still occurs in many homes today.

Picture a family with three children. Upon their graduation from high school, the father plans to honor each child with a special dinner and a gift. The first child graduates and receives a beautiful new watch. The second child is honored with dinner and a watch as well. Then the youngest in the family arrives at this important milestone and receives not dinner and a watch, but the keys to a brand new car! Not only has the father treated this third child better than the others, but he has also planted jealousy, bitterness, anger, and resentment in his other children. This is the same type of dangerous favoritism Jacob showed for Joseph. Is it any wonder his brothers hated him?

Even before the coat of many colors, the brothers knew that Joseph was not as wonderful as Jacob thought he was. Not only did he give Jacob bad reports about the brothers' behavior, on top of that, he had these dreams. The dreams were both wonderful and

If Jacob had exercised wisdom in dealing with his children, he could have done much to avoid the conflicts that developed between them.

frightening at the same time. They indicated to him that one day he would rise to a position of power over his brothers. Joseph wasted little time in sharing that prediction with them. Since they were already angry about the tunic, you can imagine that the dream business did not do much to endear him to them.

The first dream he told them was this one. All of Jacob's sons were binding sheaves in the field when Joseph's sheaf of grain rose up, and their sheaves gathered around it and bowed down to it. The brothers chided Joseph for this, and the idea that he might one day rule over them solidified their hatred for him. A more mature man might have refrained from sharing these dreams with them, but Joseph had another and told it to them too. The sun, the moon, and eleven stars all bowed down to him. He told this one to his father as well, and Jacob questioned its meaning just as the brothers had. But regardless of what they thought of these dreams, they remembered them.

Jacob compounded Joseph's already-difficult situation by asking him to check up on his brothers as they tended his flock in Shechem (see Gen. 37:12–17). He was willing to let Joseph play the role of the parent rather than take on the task himself! Notice that in Jacob's instruction he orders Joseph to check on his sons first, and then on the flock. Jacob was much more worried about his wild, unruly sons than he was a flock of stubborn, stupid sheep! But when the brothers saw "Daddy's boy" coming, they were infuriated, and they reacted violently.

*J*acob never corrected Joseph nor insisted that he stop reminding his brothers of what he had seen.

The jealousy his brothers felt toward him did not lessen with time. It seemed to intensify almost daily, until they could not stand the sight of him. Jacob never corrected Joseph nor insisted that he stop reminding his brothers of what he had seen. His brothers' sentiments were quite simple. They hated him. In fact they hated him so much, they began talking about how they might be rid of him.

Did Jacob love Joseph too much? Maybe. But his actions and his favoritism turned the hearts of the brothers against Joseph. That is certain. While they worked in the pastures, Joseph stayed at home with his father, until the fateful day that Jacob sent him to check on them and the flock they were tending. When he reached Shechem, a man found him wandering in a field and told him that the brothers had moved ahead to Dothan. So Joseph went after them and found them there. In a way, that is where his story begins.

As jealousy or hatred infects a family, the effects can be disastrous. Family relationships are complex under the best of circumstances, but when they are complicated by these negative emotions, watch out! As Joseph's brothers let their emotions run rampant, they were quickly whipped into an emotional frenzy that may have begun with "I don't like him" but ended in "Let's kill him." Since the days of Cain and Abel, these emotions have divided families and destroyed lives.

For thirteen years Americans watched family jealousies and conflicts destroy and distort the lives of the Ewing family in the popular television series *Dallas*. The Ewings, you'll remember, lived on South Fork ranch and amassed a fortune in the oil business. Jock and Ellie Ewing's two sons, J. R. and Bobby, were as different as night and day and for years were at cross purposes as they fought for control of the family business. Their struggle, brother against brother, was the backdrop for a host of personal tragedies, broken marriages, dashed careers, and shattered dreams recounted in weekly soap opera installments on television screens across America. No one, not their parents, their wives, or their friends, was able to keep these two from tearing at each other's throats.

Discipline: The Missing Ingredient

Perhaps the fictional father Jock Ewing went wrong at precisely the same point that the patriarch Jacob did: He failed early on to establish a pattern of discipline in the lives of his children. Joseph and his brothers were in control of Jacob's household in much the same way that J. R. and Bobby called the shots in the Ewing family. Both families proved the maxim that if parents do not effectively discipline their children, the task will ultimately fall to other authority figures later in life: teachers, employers, probation officers, judges.

If discipline is a key factor in successful parenting, how do we establish it in our homes? I believe we do it by dealing with our children in the same way that our Heavenly Father deals with us. God's pattern throughout the ages has been to approach man with a holy blend of law and grace, or in simple terms, limits and love. The law tells us what God is like. It defines for us His morality and His expectations. The law is an external set of parameters that we are to live within for our dealings with a holy God. Grace is a supernatural mixture of patience, help, forgiveness, and sympathy, and it is the internal expression of what our God is like. One cannot be separated from the other—His law requires what His grace provides.

This combination of law and grace as tools of discipline is beautifully illustrated in Psalm 23 by the shepherd David when he speaks of the comfort inherent in God's rod and staff. The rod was a disciplinary

Grace is a supernatural mixture of patience, help, forgiveness, and sympathy, and it is the internal expression of what our God is like.

instrument, one that enforced the "law" of the shepherd and was used to bring a wandering sheep back into the fold. The staff was also an instrument of guidance and deliverance, and used in conjunction with the rod, it kept the flock safe and secure. Both were necessary, but their functions were different.

The good parent, like the good shepherd, knows when to use each of these tools in his relationship with his children. In times of rebellion or stubborn self-will, we may need the "rod" to discipline. In times of danger we may use the staff to guide or rescue, but we can employ both knowing that they will be a continuing source of comfort to our children. Whichever instrument of discipline we employ, our children need to know that their needs, not our own, are of primary significance.

The first step of discipline as a parent is to provide a child with the parameters or guidelines that will encourage right living. Every parent wonders how to mold the will of a child without breaking his spirit—and the spirit of a child is a fragile thing. Each of us can think back to our childhood and recall incidents of correction that were especially painful. This is universal. I wonder whether there is a single person alive who has not dealt at some time with feelings of inferiority, insecurity, or inadequacy as a result of their past. But just as God the Father has done with us, we need to draw lines of correct behavior, and then help our children to meet the standards these lines define.

Where do we start? We start with guidelines established in love. As parents we must draw a consistent line, and then clearly communicate to our children where that line is. When a child chooses to cross the line we have established, he should know that there will be consequences associated with his choice. Every child is born with a will of absolute steel and with a desire to test the limits of his environment. (We're all gate checkers from time to time.) When he pushes too far and we react with anger, we frequently assume that it is our anger the child is responding to. In fact, however, children recognize that our anger indicates

*A*s parents we must draw a consistent line, and then clearly communicate to our children where that line is.

they are about to overstep the pre-drawn line, and that is why they back down. (In my years as a parent, I've discovered that children do not necessarily mind making you angry—although they do mind suffering the consequences of their disobedience!) Clearly communicated guidelines establish the groundwork for effective discipline. Beyond that the following list of do's and don't's may help.

Do use positive reinforcement

As unlikely as it may seem, children obey most of the time. Although misbehavior stands out in our minds simply because it is the exception, thankfully obedience is the norm. (If you doubt this, try using a stop watch one day to time your child's periods of disobedience; then compare that to the time that he is not misbehaving. You may be surprised!) What this means is that we parents have ample opportunity to praise our children for doing the right thing, something we don't take advantage of nearly enough. Psychologists call this positive reinforcement. Where I come from we call it giving someone an "attaboy."

If you doubt the effects of praise, try this exercise with your family. Send one person out of the room (on the first try, send an adult). Pick an object that when he returns he will need to find and move to another spot. (For example, you might want him to find a potholder in a drawer and place it on top of the refrigerator.) Call the person back into the room and tell him that he is to find some item and move it to a certain spot. Let everyone encourage him as he moves toward the item by clapping and cheering. Be silent when he is not close to it or is moving in the wrong direction. It will usually take about five minutes to successfully locate and move the item with this encouragement.

Then send that person out again and select a different item to be moved. This time communicate only negative messages to him as he tries to discover what you want him to do. Assign one family member to hit him with a rolled-up newspaper when he moves in the wrong direction. Do not cheer or clap when he is close to the item, cheer only when he is being "discouraged" in his search. You will discover that it will probably take him twice as long to successfully complete the task when given no encouragement and only discouragement.

Seize every opportunity to focus on good behavior—it is far easier to reward the good than to punish the bad. (Not to mention that it's a whole lot more fun!)

Do consider the differences in your children

A fine Bible teacher in our church likes to say, "God abandoned the cookie cutter theory when he created Adam." No two of us are alike, even when we happen to share the same parents. We would be wise to remember this truth when disciplining our children. One child may require "time out" or a spanking, while another will respond to a simple word or a look. Our oldest son, Ed, must have worn out half a dozen belts. Our middle son, Ben, got his share of spankings, too, many because he got caught doing what Ed had taught him! In contrast Cliff has marched to a different disciplinary drummer, but we wonder whether he's been better-behaved or he's just watched his brothers and learned how to better navigate around his mother and me!

When their second child arrives, many parents are shocked to find that he or she does not respond to the same cues that big brother or sister did. A wise parent understands this and becomes a student of each child, taking the time to discover the most effective means of communication for each child's particular "bent."

A **wise parent becomes a student of each child, taking the time to discover the most effective means of communication for each child's particular "bent."**

Do instruct by example

There are two ways to teach: by word and by example. The best teachers do both. Jesus was a master of this two-fold method as He spoke and lived truth before a watching world. As parents we usually depend far too much on our words and far too little on the examples we continually set for our children. But we can be sure that our actions speak at least as loudly to our children as our words. Self-discipline is the first ingredient for effective child discipline and seeing a parent live out a precept always makes a stronger impression on a child than hearing it preached.

Living by a "what's good for the kids is good for us" standard requires thought and self-control but it reaps enormous benefits. Writer Madeleine L'Engle says that her late actor-husband, Hugh Franklin, once turned down the lead role in a play after asking, "Do we want the children to see it?" The answer was no, and as parents they saw that as reason enough to decline. Discipline is easier when we hold ourselves accountable to the same standards we set for our children.

Don't discipline a child in anger

As parents we would do well to strive for the kind of control Rudyard Kipling described in his poem entitled "If": "If you can keep your head when all about you are losing theirs and blaming it on you . . ." Parenting is an emotionally charged assignment, but *if* we can control our frustration and anger when the occasion calls for discipline, our correction will be more effective.

A child who is roundly chastised by an angry parent may not be able to distinguish displeasure at his actions from displeasure with him. Acting out of anger is a reflex. Calm correction is a choice. As much as possible avoid disciplining your children in the heat of anger.

Don't discipline a child in a way that shames him

Shaming, belittling, or embarrassing a child is never a constructive means of discipline. When I was growing up the world I knew was a friendly place. Our family lived in a small town and knew most of the folks in it. I received positive "strokes" from extended family and friends, teachers, and Sunday school leaders. Today's children don't live in the same kind of environment. They face a hostile world, one where they are more likely to be torn down than built up.

> *L*et the world inflict its scars— because it will. Strive to make your home a place where discipline is administered with acceptance and love.

Christian psychiatrists Frank Minirth and Paul Meier believe that, without exception, all addictions are based on shame. What in adulthood becomes an addiction to substance or activity frequently can be traced to childhood shame. The pressure of hiding family secrets or our own perceived failures and inadequacies can be overwhelming.

The home should be a safe haven where children feel protected and nurtured. But in reality it is often a place where a child's deepest fears are realized, and he is ridiculed or shamed there more than in any other place. Let the world inflict its scars—because it will. Strive to make your home a place where discipline is administered with acceptance and love.

Don't discipline capriciously

Children have a basic need for sameness, for consistency. They don't need to wonder if they will "lose a limb" this week for an offense that we as parents "blew off" last week. Especially in correction, they need for us to maintain a standard that does not vary from day to day. Can you imagine how confusing it is for a child to be grounded for six weeks for missing a curfew, only to have the same offense ignored the next time it occurs? Being inconsistent is inconsiderate of a child's basic make-up—and it is dangerous!

Any child-rearing expert will reinforce the absolute necessity of setting a standard and holding to it. Because we are people and not computers, we will fail in this area from time to time, but consistency in discipline should be the norm that we strive for.

The final word on discipline is God's final word to us: *love*. When our Heavenly Father wanted to communicate with us, He went beyond the law and the prophets and sent the most perfect expression of love known to man, His only Son. The parent who seriously punishes a child without tears or sorrow, who does not return at a later time to express his love, has not yet understood Calvary. Love and limits. Law and grace. A good father knows that the balance is everything.

Discipline

- Expect children to challenge your authority as a parent, but don't be held hostage by misbehavior or manipulation.
- Provide an atmosphere for sibling cooperation by refusing to show favoritism for one child over another.
- Establish boundaries for your children and lovingly maintain them. Consistent discipline is a continuing source of comfort to a child.
- Explore the possibility of establishing a written code of behavior for your family. Written systems create boundaries for both parents and children.
- Be positive! Remember that children need encouragement as well as correction and can often be "caught" doing things right.
- Always discipline with love as your primary motivation. Children need to know they are loved, even when they are being corrected.

Chapter 5

Looking Up Through the Darkness

Surviving Adversity

Now when they saw him afar off, even before he came near them, they conspired against him to kill him. Then they said to one another, "Look, this dreamer is coming! Come therefore, let us now kill him and cast him into some pit; and we shall say, 'Some wild beast has devoured him.' We shall see what will become of his dreams!" But Reuben heard it, and he delivered him out of their hands, and said, "Let us not kill him." And Reuben said to them, "Shed no blood, but cast him into this pit which is in the wilderness, and do not lay a hand on him"—that he might deliver him out of their hands and bring him back to his father. So it came to pass, when Joseph had come to his brothers, that they stripped Joseph of his tunic, the tunic of many colors that was on him. Then they took him and cast him into a pit.

Genesis 37:18–24a

Looking Up Through the Darkness

Lots of folks today romanticize the period in our country's history known as the Great Depression. Through the scrim of forty-odd years the struggle of many families to carve out all but the simplest existence has taken on a kind of rosy hue. Television helped to soften the memory further in the seventies with Earl Hamner's nostalgic creation of the Waltons, a family who loved each other through the hard times and reflected a glowing picture of bucolic living in the midst of poverty. Many in my generation like to point to our own "hungry years" and recall how they brought us closer. But the truth is, hard times are hard on families because they're hard on people.

*A*s Christians we have the assurance from the Word of God that suffering is a part of His teaching curriculum for our lives, and that it is not an elective!

We're better insulated today from the forces that make life difficult than our ancestors were. We have central air conditioning and central heat to regulate the temperature of our environment. We have modern conveniences that can provide us with instant meals so that important time need not be spent in the kitchen. We have security systems that guard our homes and our possessions and investment counselors who guard our financial future. What we don't have, however, is the security of knowing that we will never have to suffer pain or loss. In fact, as

Christians we have the opposite assurance from the Word of God that suffering is a part of His teaching curriculum for our lives, and that it is not an elective!

In the musical *Fiddler on the Roof,* Tevya laments the suffering and hardship the Jewish people have experienced throughout history. Looking up to heaven he implores, "Lord, I know we are your chosen people . . . but couldn't you choose someone else the next time?" If the option were left open to most of us, like Tevya we'd skip the hard times and the hungry years. But in God's economy hardships are not only predictable, they are actually profitable!

When young Joseph set out to find his brothers who were tending Jacob's herds in Dothan, it's doubtful that he anticipated the disaster that awaited him. He knew that his brothers resented his very presence. When he found them at Dothan, they had already conspired against him and plotted his murder. As soon as they saw him coming, they nudged one another and said, "Here comes the dreamer!" Their initial plan was to kill him on the spot, throw him in a pit, and tell Jacob that a wild animal had devoured him. For some reason Joseph would never understand, Reuben (of all people) talked the others out of it. He suggested that instead they simply throw Joseph into the pit, but not kill him. (Maybe Reuben planned to rescue Joseph later, but subsequent events prevented that possibility.)

They seized Joseph, stripped his prized tunic from him, and threw him into an empty pit. Then they sat down beside the pit and calmly ate their lunches! Joseph begged their mercy, but they left him in the dark pit to die. The dreamer was stuck in a dark place with no one but God! As you can see, there was no love lost between Joseph and his brothers at this point. As they were picnicking, a caravan of Ishmaelites on their way to Egypt passed by with camels bearing sweet gum and spices. Seeing more profit in a live slave than a dead brother, the brothers decided then and there to sell Joseph into slavery to the Ishmaelites. (The sale was Judah's idea, but the others readily agreed.) They pulled him up out of the pit, and sold him to the Ishmaelite traders for thirty shekels of silver.

What a strange experience. Joseph overheard his brothers planning to tell his father that he had been killed. And he knew from what he heard his new "owners" saying that he would travel far from home and would probably never return. The course of life can change radically in a moment, can't it? Joseph's did on that day.

His brothers went to great lengths to convince their father of his death. They took his tunic (which Jacob knew Joseph would never have given up) and dipped it in the blood of a slaughtered male goat. When they arrived back at home they handed it to Jacob with these words: "We found this; please examine it to see whether it is your son's tunic or not."

Before he even turned it over in his hands, Jacob knew the garment was Joseph's. He voiced the meaning of their charade before they had a chance to explain, saying, "A wild beast has devoured him; Joseph has surely been torn to pieces!" In the traditional expression of emotion, Jacob tore his own coat in grief, put sackcloth on his body, and mourned for days on end. No matter who tried to comfort him, he would not be quieted. He wept bitterly and grieved over the loss, unaware that Joseph was still very much alive.

What happened to Joseph is not hard to explain. Why? Because a godly person seeking to live a life of purity in the home, the workplace, or anywhere will always be under fire from the godless. Centuries after Joseph's brothers threw him in the pit to starve, the apostle Paul wrote these words to his young friend Timothy: "Indeed, all who desire to live godly in Christ Jesus will be persecuted." In other words, hard times are inevitable!

Graduates from the School of Suffering

Have you ever spent a night in a pit with no one but God? Has someone you loved left you there? Welcome to Suffering 101—God's boot camp for would-be saints.

Joseph's darkest hour came as ours frequently do—unexpectedly, and on the heels of much happiness, security, and success. He was a favored son, a young man touched by the hand of God with dreams of a bright future. How often that is the case. Job, another Old Testament character with a first-hand experience with suffering, met with shattering trials that followed great blessing. He was known as a blameless, upright man—a family man with seven sons and three daughters and incredible wealth: "Also, his possessions were 7,000 sheep, 3,000 camels, 500 yoke of oxen, 500 female donkeys, and a very large household, so that this man was the greatest of all the people of the East" (Job 1:3).

Joseph's darkest hour came as ours frequently do—unexpectedly, and on the heels of much happiness, security, and success.

David is another example of great failure that followed tremendous success. Anointed king of Israel as a young boy by the prophet Samuel, he won an incredible victory over the Philistine giant Goliath and then spent the next ten years on the run from his mentor-turned-enemy, Saul, who tried every chance he got to kill David. The Scriptures are full of stories of men and women of faith who conquered—and who suffered. The writer of Hebrews chronicles many of them:

> And what more shall I say? For the time would fail me to tell of Gideon and Barak and Samson and Jephthah, also of David and Samuel and the prophets: who through faith subdued kingdoms, worked righteousness, obtained promises, stopped the mouths of lions, quenched the violence of fire, escaped the edge of the sword, out of weakness were made strong, became valiant in battle,

turned to flight the armies of the aliens. Women
received their dead raised to life again.

Hebrews 11:32–35

Now watch carefully:

Others were tortured, not accepting deliverance,
that they might obtain a better resurrection. Still
others had trial of mockings and scourgings, yes,
and of chains and imprisonment. They were
stoned, they were sawn in two, were tempted, were
slain with the sword. They wandered about in
sheepskins and goatskins, being destitute, af-
flicted, tormented—of whom the world was not
worthy. They wandered in deserts and mountains,
in dens and caves of the earth.

Hebrews 11:35–38

Most importantly, suffering should not surprise us because it marked
the life of our Savior. Again, the author of Hebrews writes:

Though He was a Son, yet He learned obedience
by the things which He suffered. And having been
perfected, He became the author of eternal salvation to all who obey Him.

Hebrews 5:8–9

Suffering taught the Son of God obedience, and it perfected Him as our
Savior and the source of our salvation. The same God/man who experienced
the elation of a parade in His honor on Palm Sunday suffered (just a few

short days later) the anguish of total surrender in Gethsemane and the brutal pain of death on Calvary.

Bridge or Barrier?

We're all familiar with the cliché, "When the going gets tough, the tough get going." But for many of us that phrase is incomplete. It should continue, "the tough get going in the opposite direction!" So often we retreat from the tough times and question the plan of a God who would allow our particular pain. But He is not a wasteful Father or a cruel one. Suffering presents us with a personal challenge. We can use our suffering as a bridge in building relationships with others, or we can view it as a wall that separates us from those around us. The choice is ours.

*W*e can use our suffering as a bridge in building relationships with others, or we can view it as a wall that separates us from those around us.

Shortly after I came to Houston as pastor of Second Baptist Church, I met Stanley and Diane Williams, who had lost a daughter in a tragic automobile accident years before. To this day they are among the first to go to any home where there is a similar tragedy because they can listen and minister like no one else can. No pastor on our staff could ever surpass the validity and compassion of this couple's consolation because they have been there, and they have chosen to use their experience to minister to others.

A Future and a Hope

Brenda and George Hederhorst's twelve-year-old daughter, Shannon, died inexplicably in her sleep on December 16, 1977, never having shown any symptoms of the acute diabetes that caused her death. Because it was so close to the Christmas holidays, Brenda and George and their two younger daughters immersed themselves in seasonal activities to help get through the initial shock of their devastating loss. In the weeks that followed friends came in a steady stream, bringing meals and comfort.

Until this tragedy occurred Brenda had lived what many would call a charmed life. She was reared by godly parents, accepted Christ as her Savior as a young girl of ten, and married her college sweetheart, who was a fine Christian man. She was steadfastly convinced that God's promise in Jeremiah 29:11 was hers, that He had a plan for her life and her future was one of hope, not misfortune.

When Shannon died, Brenda met with grief in a profoundly personal way. Because she had not experienced such loss before, she began reading books about others who had lost children. Friends continued to pray for this family as they struggled to put their lives together again. As God healed their hearts He also built into them a compassion for others who had experienced similar loss. In their own tragedy they learned God is totally sufficient, and because of His sufficiency, we can be totally dependent on Him.

Today George and Brenda minister to families who have lost children through a support group in our church called "Lost and Found." They are uniquely equipped for this ministry in a way few are because they have lived through a similar loss and emerged whole on the other side. People who meet Brenda today are often surprised to learn her story. She is not bitter nor does she question God's wisdom. Instead, she thanks Him for twelve wonderful years with her oldest daughter. When people ask how many children she has, her frequent answer is "Three. One in heaven with Jesus, and two here on earth with us."

These real-life testimonies cast a new light on the apostle Paul's words when he said that the God of all comfort "comforts us in all our tribulation, that we may be able to comfort those who are in any trouble, with the comfort with which we ourselves are comforted by God" (2 Cor. 1:4).

It's Just Not Fair!

Joseph could have asked God why the hard times came, but he didn't. He could have become bitter and angry about his circumstances, but he didn't, not even after his brothers threw him in a pit and then sold him for the equivalent of fifteen dollars (the price of an old, unfit slave) to a band of traders on their way to Egypt. When they reached Egypt they sold Joseph to a man named Potiphar, who was an officer of Pharaoh and the captain of his bodyguard. Joseph never dreamed he would be a slave! He never expected to leave the security of his father's house. Egypt was new and strange. But the hours he had spent in the pit earlier were the beginning of a new life for Joseph.

In Potiphar's household, Joseph found himself in a position of power, and the object of Potiphar's wife's desire! When she falsely accused him of sexually assaulting her, he landed in prison and languished there for years before being summoned by Pharaoh. Was it fair? No way! But the secret of surviving suffering and tragedy is learning to see things God's way. Later, Joseph was able to look back and thank God for the time he spent looking up through the darkness of the pit.

Elisabeth Elliot, widow of murdered missionary Jim Elliot, expressed it this way: "God is God. I dethrone Him in my heart when I demand that He act in ways that satisfy my idea of justice." Jim Elliot had been her husband for little more than two years when his untimely death left her to raise their baby daughter alone in a strange country. Yet she adamantly refused to condemn or question God for the circumstances of her particular pain.

Perhaps you've been in the pit. Maybe you're waiting in a dark, windowless place now. There are a host of things that can land the sturdiest of us there, from illness or death to the loss of a job, financial ruin, separation, or divorce. Perhaps your personal pit is so deep and dark that it has caused you to question God's very existence. If so, take heart in this basic biblical principle: *Those whom God would greatly use and bless will always experience a time of suffering.* It is not possible to be significantly used by God in any area of endeavor without suffering. In fact, suffering seems to be the prerequisite for God's blessings.

> *It* is not possible to be significantly used by God in any area of endeavor without suffering.

When Life Is the Pits!

Following Joseph's unjust imprisonment for an alleged sexual assault on Potiphar's wife, he became a model prisoner. His behavior was so exemplary that he was eventually given charge over all the other prisoners. I believe Joseph learned three significant things during those years in the dungeon, lessons that you and I can apply to our own pits or prison experiences of suffering.

Cling tenaciously to God no matter what

Joseph wasn't counting on family, friends, or his former employer to correct the injustices of his life. He was counting on God to redeem them.

Joseph should have been able to count on his brothers not to sell him into slavery, but they let him down. He should have been able to count on his cell-mate, the chief butler, to keep his word and remember Joseph when he was released, yet "the chief butler did not remember Joseph, but forgot him" (Gen. 40:23). He might have hoped that Potiphar's wife would reconsider her false claim and confirm his innocence, but she never did. Joseph wasn't counting on family, friends, or his former employer to correct the injustices of his life. He was counting on God to redeem them. If we wait to be rescued by the people we depend on, we will usually be disappointed.

The secret Joseph learned in his suffering was total dependence to God and God alone. That is the cornerstone of a strong foundation for living. Our primary responsibility is to cling to Him. It is almost as if God were saying, "You take care of the depth of your life, laying the strong foundation of a personal relationship with Me, and in My sovereign power I'll take care of the height, the length, and the breadth of your life."

Rest in the knowledge that God is faithful

Joseph languished in prison for two years following the chief butler's promise to put in a good word for him. Every time he heard the rattle of keys or the creak of a cell door he must have thought, "This is it! They're finally coming for me! The butler has worked out my release at last." But the days turned into weeks, the weeks to months, and eventually the months became years. It began to look as though he might never be released, but Joseph still rested in the faithfulness of God.

Francis Schaeffer says that when we lack proper contentment we have either ceased to believe that God is God, or we have failed to be submissive to Him. Believing that God is God requires believing in His

Waiting gracefully is the mark of a true saint.

faithfulness because that faithfulness is an essential part of His character. Our confidence in God is much like that of the little girl who crawled up into her father's lap while he was reading the newspaper and told him how much she wanted him to build her a dollhouse. She didn't climb down until her daddy had promised to do just that, although he was somewhat distracted and agreed mostly because he wanted to be allowed to continue reading his paper. He forgot his promise until he walked into her room one evening and saw all her dolls and doll furniture were packed to move into the new dollhouse. When he asked her about it, she simply told him that she knew he would be building it (even though he hadn't yet begun!) because he had promised that he would. That was good enough for her.

Joseph knew that the God he served is a God who keeps His promises. Because He is changeless, we know that He is still in the business of keeping them today. Deuteronomy 32:4 says, "His work is perfect; / For all His ways are justice, / A God of truth and without injustice; / righteous and upright is He." We can rest in that faithfulness even when uncertainty surrounds us.

Wait on God

I can't think of a single thing more difficult to do than wait. Most skills can be improved with constant practice, but waiting is one that doesn't seem to get any easier no matter how much experience we gain. Waiting gracefully is the mark of a true saint. Some might argue that Joseph had little choice but to wait out his prison experience, but most of us wait in places that seem to beg us to do something, anything, that will circumvent the need to wait on God.

David, the psalmist, wrote these words years after Joseph's ordeal: "Wait for the Lord and keep His way, and He will exalt you to inherit the land" (Ps. 37:34 NASV). How difficult waiting is. The temptation to jump ahead of God is irresistible at times, especially when it seems that He is not concerned with our very pressing present circumstances. My friend Jeannette Clift George, a gifted actress and speaker, likes to say with a chuckle that God is never late, although He has missed numerous good opportunities to be early. The fact of the matter is, He is always on time—His perfect time.

The Three P's of God's School in Suffering

If Joseph could, I think he'd advise us to use the experience of unjust suffering for all it's worth! His life is proof that hardships can be overcome and that they are a useful part of God's plan for perspective, for preservation, and for preparation.

Perspective

There's nothing like a dose of pain to give us a different view of life. Through suffering we manage to see the essentials of our existence more clearly. We come to understand with more certainty what really matters, and what doesn't. And we begin to see that, rather than being "picked on" by God, we are simply facing what countless others, godly and ungodly, have faced. As Charles Dickens wrote in the classic *David Copperfield*, "Accidents will occur in the best regulated families." And they do.

Years after he spent a dark night in the pit, Joseph reached the point where he could thank God for the experience. Finally he could say, "Lord, thank You for the pit. Thank You for allowing me to be a slave. Thank You for the false accusations of Mrs. Potiphar. Thank You for putting me in that dungeon, where I could meet two VIPs. Lord, thank You for those two years that I waited in prison before I was remembered. While I'm at it, Lord, thank You for all the injustices of my life, for I know they've made me what You meant for me to be!"

*I*f we always had smooth sailing we would never know the utter sufficiency and sovereignty of the God we serve.

If we always had smooth sailing we would never know the utter sufficiency and sovereignty of the God we serve. It is often through suffering that our perspective is widened and we see His overwhelming power in our lives.

Preservation

When the ground around San Francisco shook, rumbled, and broke open in September 1989, Americans held their breath as they watched televised reports of devastation and death. Rescue workers labored for days to save those trapped in the wreckage of buildings, freeways, and automobiles. Days after the quake, when all hope for survivors had dissolved, these same workers, who by this time had seen much tragedy, wept with joy and weary relief at the sight of one man, miraculously preserved, pulled from the heap of twisted metal and pulverized brick that had once been his home. When life falls to pieces around us, God preserves.

Scientist and inventor Thomas Edison was sixty-seven years old and at the pinnacle of his career when his laboratory facility caught fire. Edison's son remembers shouting for his father as the fire raged out of control, not knowing if he was trapped inside. As he cried out he saw his father running toward him saying, "Son, go get your mother and bring her here. She'll never see another fire like this one as long as she lives." While the fire was still burning, Edison leaned back on a table and fell asleep. The next day he called together all his employees and said, "We're starting over. This time we're going to make it better than before. We're going to build it from scratch and do it right." As he sifted through the ashes of his office, Edison found a picture of himself, frayed and charred around the edges but with the image still intact. Picking up the picture he turned to his son and said, "See, the fire never touched me. It never touched me."

*I*t's easy to see how joy and success prepare us, but it's a little harder to understand how our loving God uses pain as an instrument too.

We may lose all we have acquired materially in this life, but if we have invested in spiritual values, no tragedy that can happen in this fallen world will ever touch us. The beloved hymn "Amazing Grace" says it best: "Through many dangers toils and snares, I have already come; 'Tis grace hath brought me safe thus far, and grace will lead me home."

Preparation

I could bore you to death with the story of my life. I could tell you how I sold subscriptions to the New Orleans *Times Picayune* one summer, or how I painted house numbers on curbs, or how I sold men's clothing. I have worked in a coal mine, surveyed land, set off dynamite for tunneling, and wired houses for electricity. I could tell you countless stories about my mother, father and brother, aunts and uncles, friends, and old girlfriends. But I am convinced that as boring as these details might seem to you, strung together they would reflect the supernatural work of God in my life and His preparation for what He has called me to do today. God has used every moment, every success, every failure in my life to this point to equip me for His service.

It's easy to see how joy and success prepare us, but it's a little harder to understand how our loving God uses pain as an instrument too. A family in our church owns a wild game ranch in the Texas hill country. Many species of exotic and endangered animals reside on this ranch, and among them there is none more awkward-looking to me than the giraffe. Now I've never seen a giraffe being born, but I hear it's really something. The first parts to emerge are the baby giraffe's front hooves and head. Then the entire calf appears and tumbles ten feet to the ground, landing on its back. Within a matter of seconds, he rolls over and stands, struggling with untried legs. Then an amazing thing happens. The mother giraffe positions herself directly over her newborn calf and looks it over. Then she swings her long leg outward and kicks her baby, sending it sprawling head-over-heels. If it doesn't get up, she repeats the violent assault. If it grows tired, she kicks it again to stimulate its efforts. Each time the baby giraffe manages to get to its feet, its mother kicks it over again! It seems incredibly cruel doesn't it? But the mother is simply preparing her little calf for survival. He must learn to get up quickly and run with the herd away from danger, or he will be easy prey and perish.

His Is a Heart We Can Trust

In her lovely song, entitled "Trust His Heart," singer-songwriter Babbie Mason says, "God is too wise to be mistaken; God is too good to be unkind. So when you don't understand, when you don't see His plan, when you can't trace His hand, trust His heart." Until we go through a period of privation, suffering, and difficulty, we cannot fully appreciate the blessings of God when they arrive. Trust that He is preparing you and me for all the days and hours ahead—days that hold challenges and rewards only He can clearly see.

Adversity

- Christians are not immune from hard times—in fact, we're guaranteed them! Even the Son of God suffered and learned from the experience.
- We can allow our suffering to become a bridge to others or a barrier in our relationships with them and with God. The choice is ours.
- Those whom God would greatly use and bless are almost always those who have experienced great suffering.
- When adversity comes, cling to God, rest in the knowledge that He is faithful, and ask Him for the strength to wait for His blessing.

Chapter 6

Keep the Change!

Dealing with Change

Now Joseph had been taken down to Egypt. And Potiphar, an officer of Pharaoh, captain of the guard, an Egyptian, bought him from the Ishmaelites who had taken him down there. The LORD was with Joseph, and he was a successful man; and he was in the house of his master the Egyptian. And his master saw that the LORD was with him and that the LORD made all he did to prosper in his hand. So Joseph found favor in his sight, and served him. Then he made him overseer of his house and all that he had, that the LORD blessed the Egyptian's house for Joseph's sake; and the *blessing of the LORD was on all that he had in the house and in the field.*

Genesis 39:1–5

Dealing with Change

Joseph's life in Egypt was marked by change. Nothing about that land was like his homeland. There was a multitude of adjustments to make in this new place, not the least of which was becoming a servant in another man's household. His master, Potiphar, was the captain of the bodyguard and a very important man in Egypt, second only to Pharaoh himself. Only one thing from Joseph's old life remained constant in his new one: God never left him. Even in the midst of tremendous change, God's presence was there. Joseph knew it, and Potiphar knew it too.

I believe God's presence was the reason Joseph found favor with Potiphar. Everything he touched seemed to prosper, and in a short time Potiphar made Joseph his personal servant and overseer of his household. He placed Joseph in charge of everything he owned. Imagine! A foreigner, a son of Abraham, managing the affairs of an important Egyptian!

From the time Potiphar appointed Joseph overseer, God blessed his house. Everything he owned, in the house and in the fields, prospered as never before. It was as if God were saying to Joseph, "I know where you are, Joseph, and I am the One who cares for you." Potiphar was amazed at his foreign slave and at the power and might of Joseph's God. You don't get to be one of the most powerful men in Egypt by being a fool, and Potiphar knew a good thing when he saw it. Before long he put everything he owned in Joseph's charge and never again concerned himself with anything except the food he ate!

> *I*t was as if God were saying to Joseph, "I know where you are, Joseph, and I am the One who cares for you."

Joseph was homesick at times. Potiphar's house was beautiful and Egypt was a land of great riches, but he longed for his home. He'd had a family once. Now he lived with strangers. Everything was different—the food, the language, the customs. It was all new to him! But the greatest pain of his heart came when he remembered his father, and Benjamin, and wondered if they had forgotten him.

When the homesickness was almost unbearable, Joseph would remind himself of God's provision in Egypt. No, it was not his home. But his God and the God of his fathers had traveled with him to this place and remained with him even in the midst of despair. He might have been a slave, but he had a trusting and lenient master. He might have been lonely, but he was seldom alone. Even the changes themselves were full of challenge, and there were countless things to learn and master in his new home.

Sometimes he marveled at Potiphar's trust. What did he see? Joseph was bright but not brilliant. He was honest but not above all reproach. He had some natural abilities but nothing to warrant the faith Potiphar so readily placed in him. Probably, Potiphar simply saw God's workmanship, the only truly extraordinary thing Joseph brought from Canaan.

Keep the Change!

The Reckoning sounds like a book on theology, but it isn't. It's a book about change, and it was written by an observer of the automobile industry who says that many of America's major corporations are in serious trouble today because they refuse to change with the times. IBM, General Motors, and Sears are among the companies cited that missed the wave of change years ago and have played catch up in the marketplace ever since.

The lessons of *The Reckoning* apply to individuals as well as businesses. We live in a fast-moving society, and to survive and grow we have to move with it. We cannot be satisfied with the status quo, nor can we live in yesterday. Change is the very stuff of life. God created, and the universe has been in motion ever since. The smallest particle of life we know, the atom, is energy in its simplest form. Heat and light are waves that move through space, and they are never still. Our bodies are constantly changing as we age, although we've gotten pretty good at disguising that fact. (A physicist once said, "Look at me in a hurry because I'm changing rapidly.")

Although it seems a contradiction, change is one of the most consistent things in life. We can always count on it. Joseph went through incredible changes in his life before he was thirty years of age. His mother died when he was a young boy. He was taken out of his home and sold as a slave and then taken away to a foreign culture where he knew no one. He became familiar with the ups and downs of life, moving from a palace to a prison and back. He was in favor and then unjustly accused, forgotten and then remembered.

I remember as if it were yesterday the day Jo Beth and I put up a little high chair and turned our kitchen "table for two" into a table for three. Before long we had to move our first son, Ed, out of the high chair to make room for Ben. Then a few years went by and Cliff was born. We added a fifth chair. It seemed just a short time later that Ed graduated from high school and went off to college, and then there were four chairs around the table again. Ed finished seminary, got married, and our granddaughter was born. Then Ben left home for college and, after that, seminary. So Ben's chair "left" the table. Ben married just a few weeks before Cliff graduated from high school. Now Jo Beth and I are back to our table for two. Naturally, children grow up and leave the nest. We expect that change, and yet it seems to happen so quickly!

Change is one of the most consistent things in life, but it has the potential to become a crisis if we are unprepared or unable to adjust to it.

Change is one of the most consistent things in life, but it has the potential to become a crisis if we are unprepared or unable to adjust to it.

Whether expected or unexpected, change has the potential to become a crisis if we are unprepared or unable to adjust to it. Psychologists tell us that sudden changes, such as a death, serious illness, relocation, loss of a job, or even a job promotion, can threaten not only personal stability, but the stability of our most intimate relationships as well. But change does not have to be life-altering for us to resist it. Even the slightest change can be uncomfortable for us. I can illustrate this principle with a simple exercise. Fold your hands together, lacing your fingers as if you were praying. Now move each of your fingers just one digit over and fold them again. It feels strange doesn't it? We often find ourselves similarly uncomfortable or "out of joint" when faced with the slightest change in our lives.

Some Truths About Change

Change is relentless

An old fellow had been in the north woods for weeks by himself, camping out. Each night at dusk he built a campfire, boiled water for coffee, and took out his skillet to fry up some bacon for dinner. As he was sitting by the fire one night, the water boiling and the bacon sizzling, he heard a tremendous racket in the brush. The sound was like a roaring freight train, and as trees fell over and branches snapped, the biggest bear he'd ever seen lumbered into the clearing. On the bear's back was a tough-looking hombre holding a seven-foot live rattlesnake in his hands.

The man shouted and screamed as he brought the bear to a skidding halt, bit the head off the rattlesnake, and flung it into the brush. Then he slid off the bear's back, turned, and hit him between the eyes, knocking him unconscious. The camper was speechless as this wild-eyed renegade walked over to the fire, tossed the boiling coffee down his throat, drank the hot grease from the skillet, and ate all of the bacon in one bite. As he wiped his hands with poison ivy and slapped the bear back to consciousness, he turned to the camper and said, "Partner, I'm sorry I can't stay around and visit with you a while, but I've got to keep moving 'cause a real bad dude is chasing me!"

No matter how tough we are, we are vulnerable to change. It is always there nipping at our heels, urging us to keep moving forward. The world never stops changing, even if we stop changing with it.

Change is risky

There's a comfort in doing things the way they've always been done. When Moses died he was the only leader the nation of Israel had ever known. They were at the Jordan River on the edge of the promised land, and the reins of authority had been turned over to Joshua. God's direction to Joshua was to get up, take the people, and cross the river into Canaan. There was just one problem. The people didn't want to go.

Moses was the one who had made the decisions. Moses had performed the miracles. Moses had led the wandering Israelites through crisis after crisis. But now Moses was dead. Pessimistic, despairing, and complaining, they wanted to go back to Egypt rather than move on without their familiar leader.

This same resistance to the risk of change has been true in other eras and with other peoples. During the American Revolution there were colonists who would rather put up with the oppressive yoke of unrepresentative taxation than fight for a new freedom. Fighting presented the risk of losing, and that was a risk many did not want to take. During the Renaissance and the Reformation (times of tremendous, creative change) there were those whose rallying cry was "give me the status quo." But the world will never be changed by men and women who say "make mine the same."

The world will never be changed by men and women who say "make mine the same."

George Bernard Shaw said, "The reasonable man adapts himself to the world; the unreasonable one persists in trying to adapt the world to himself. Therefore, all progress depends on the unreasonable man." Thank God for all the unreasonable men who have embraced change and made our world a better place, in spite of the inherent risks.

Change is painful

Our church has an affiliated private school for children in kindergarten through twelfth grade, and one of the "liveliest" days on our campus each year is the first day of school. On that fall morning, the place to be to observe most of the "action" is in the kindergarten or first grade rooms. Great change is going on. Children are leaving the secure, familiar environment of the home and facing the prospect of a new place, new faces, new challenges.

The fact that some tears are shed on that first day should not surprise anyone. Change can be painful. By the way, the children are not the only ones who cry. The mother who sends her child off to school for the first time knows that in some way things will never be the same again. A process of growth and blossoming independence has begun that is necessary and good, but nevertheless painful.

We make significant changes every year in the Bible study program of our church. Because the tendency is for a class to get "overloaded" with leadership as it grows, we've instituted a process we call "the draft" to re-distribute leaders and strengthen all classes for the good of the overall program. The first year we "drafted" we had a lot of angry folks. Most people liked things just the way they were and resisted the interference. They were comfortable with the status quo. Many leadership teams found it painful to break up, but the genius of the draft is that this kind of change helps to build a stronger body of Christ. It's radical and it doesn't always feel good. But it works!

Change is painful—building new relationships, moving to new places, getting involved in new endeavors—these things can hurt. But the alternative to change is stagnation and death, a high price for temporary comfort!

God's Place in Change

What is God's position in the midst of our changing circumstances? It can be described in two words: immutable and sovereign. To say that God is immutable is to say He never changes. Hebrews 13:8 says that Jesus Christ is the same yesterday, today, and forever. His Word does not change. His character does not change. God's message of love and salvation through His Son Jesus Christ does not change.

In his book *The 7 Habits of Highly Effective People,* Stephen R. Covey says that having something changeless anchors us in the midst of a changing world. "People can't live with change if there's not a changeless core inside of them," he says. "The key to the ability to change is a changeless sense of who you are, and what you are about and what you value."[1] The "changeless core" inside the believer is Christ Himself, our hope of glory. He is the rock that we can cling to when nothing else seems secure.

God is not only immutable, He is sovereign. This means that God is always working out His will, His plan, His purpose, His dreams in every realm of life. His plan for the destiny of mankind is being put forth in the everyday affairs of men, or otherwise this whole thing would be hopeless! Some believe we live in a world that turns on the spin of a roulette wheel, on luck, or chance. That is not true. God is operating in our world, a fact Paul explained to the church at Colossae saying, "For by Him all things were created that are in heaven and that are on earth, visible and invisible, whether thrones or dominions or principalities or powers. All things were created through Him and for Him. And He is before all things, *and in Him all things consist* (Col. 1:16–17, italics added).

> *The "changeless core" inside the believer is Christ Himself, our hope of glory.*

What Are Our Options in the Face of Change?

The key to surviving and thriving in an atmosphere of change is *perspective*. We can view change in one of several ways, but the view we choose will determine whether change becomes an obstacle or an opportunity for us.

We can view change in one of several ways, but the view we choose will determine whether change becomes an obstacle or an opportunity for us.

We can choose resistance

One response to change is to fight it. Sears, one of the leading retailers in America, resisted market pressure to change their way of doing business for many years. In 1970 Sears stock was $62 a share, but at one point in 1980 it traded for as low as $14. As their percentage of retail sales declined, Sears executives began examining possible causes for the drop. This operational "gut check" revealed layer upon layer of unnecessary bureaucracy (including over forty top executives in the drapery area alone!) and a growing insensitivity to the marketplace. We can resist change around us, but that resistance draws a costly penalty. We fall behind those who are more willing to change, and instead of leading, we find ourselves in the position of playing catch up.

We can choose resignation

To simply resign oneself to change is to take the position of a martyr. "There is nothing I can do about this, so I'll just let it roll right over me." This choice differs from resistance because essentially it is passive. Those who merely resign themselves to change take a *que sera, sera* attitude toward life, believing they are at the mercy of their circumstances. And as long as an attitude of resignation prevails, a person's circumstances *do* determine his fate.

*R*e-scripting in the face of change is a shifting of our way of looking at it.

We can choose removal

When children play and things do not go their way their "ace in the hole" is to stop the game and go home. If change is too threatening we too can choose to exit the game by removing ourselves or changing our environment. Mental hospitals are filled with people who have simply removed themselves from life because they found its twists and turns too difficult. Many marriages fail because two people who promised to be committed to one another "for better or for worse" don't want to deal with the constant changes of matrimony. Opting out is a last ditch option. If we remove ourselves from the changes of life, we stop growing. And when we stop growing, we die.

Each of the three perspectives on change we've looked at so far view change as an obstacle. There is another perspective we can choose that makes change not an obstacle but an opportunity.

We can choose to re-script

Re-scripting in the face of change is a shifting of our way of looking at it. Recently I saw an interview with former San Francisco Giants' pitcher

Dave Dravecky that illustrated this kind of courageous choice. Dravecky's story is one of the most inspirational sports testimonies I know of. Tests on a lump on Dravecky's left arm in January 1988 indicated that it was probably benign. But nine months later doctors believed the lump was malignant and recommended a biopsy. The results of the testing were positive.

In October 1988 Dravecky underwent surgery to remove one-half of the deltoid muscle in his pitching arm. A portion of the bone in his arm was frozen to kill any remaining cancer cells. Less than a year later Dravecky was pitching again in the minor leagues—a feat his doctors considered miraculous.

In August 1989 he pitched his first major league game in over a year, going eight innings against the Cincinnati Reds and winning 4-3. Before he threw his first pitch (while he was still in the bullpen!), 34,810 fans rose to their feet in thunderous applause. It was an unforgettable moment in the history of sports, but it was by no means the end of the Dave Dravecky story.

Five days later while pitching in Montreal, his humerus bone snapped, and in October 1989 it broke again during a victory celebration in the National League championship series. He announced his retirement from baseball in the next month. The cancer returned in 1991, and finally the doctors had to amputate Dravecky's left arm. Viewers watching an interview with the former player following this latest life-changing surgery heard him say that the two years of heartbreaking setbacks and thrilling victories had prepared him for the loss of his arm. He refused to ask God why, but remained convinced that He had a plan for his life and that his most recent surgery was a part of it. He was upbeat and positive, thrilled to be alive and eager for what God had in store for him. Dave Dravecky re-scripted a change many would have considered a tragedy. All the other options in response to this roller coaster ride of change were available to him, but he chose to see his circumstances as a doorway to different opportunities.

Change is the hallmark of family life. Marriage, the beginning of a new family unit, is a tremendous change from the single lifestyle. The birth of a child alters the balance of a marriage, bringing a third person and new relationships into the equation. As other children are born, the picture becomes more complex. Careers advance, stall, or decline, bringing changes in the family's standard of living.

Later in life, aging parents may require long-term medical care and an avalanche of decisions must be made concerning their well-being. Homes are purchased and sold, businesses are started, and college educations are planned and funded. Then children marry and grandchildren are born, expanding the family circle even farther. Even without the intrusion of great tragedy or unexpected fortune, the landscape of family living is constantly marked by change. But at times the unexpected does occur and requires a special kind of perspective for survival.

Viewing Crisis as Opportunity

Ron and Jan Kircus are a fine young couple who married in their mid-twenties. Both had been involved in the singles ministry of our church and served faithfully in other areas as well. When they married in the early 1980s, Ron was selling oilfield pipe, and with his personable manner, drive, and attention to detail he did very well in that business.

The **landscape of family living is constantly marked by change.**

As Ron continued to grow in the Lord, he became aware that God was leading him into full-time ministry. This was quite a vocational change and one that he had never anticipated, but he and Jan began to pray that God would lead them in the way He had prepared. During this time they learned that Jan was pregnant, and they began to prepare with great anticipation for yet another change.

As a deacon in our church Ron was often "in the trenches," serving faithfully in one behind-the-scenes capacity or another. One such occasion for service had a life-changing impact on Ron and his family. Our church moved into new worship facilities in the summer of 1986. As you might imagine such a move involved hundreds of small tasks to make our members and guests feel at home in the new surroundings. Large banners were made to direct visitors to available parking on our campus, and on a hot Saturday afternoon in June, Ron and his good friend Kirk were hanging a banner in the parking lot south of our new worship center.

Using a hydraulic ladder, Ron and Kirk worked together to secure the banner. The banner was almost hung when Ron prepared to go up the ladder again. Kirk remembers that he offered to go instead, but Ron insisted he would go because he was already sweaty from the last trip. This time the ladder tilted and came crashing four stories to the ground with Ron in its cage. He took the full impact of the fall on his face—a fact doctors would later tell him saved his life.

Ron remembers very little about the next hours and he still considers that a blessing. His doctors performed surgery, unsure that he would live through the night. Jan kept a constant vigil with family and friends, aware that the child she was carrying might never know his father. Miraculously, Ron survived. Using the same determination he had previously applied to his work, he began the long and painful process of recovery. In the beginning he had little memory. There were times he could not remember who Jan was. When co-workers visited, he would have to ask someone else who had been to see him.

Ron worked for a full year to get back the physical and mental capabilities that the accident took away. Hours of therapy and months of progressing from wheelchair to walker to cane were necessary to do this. Six months after his fall Jan and Ron had a son they named Sam. Ron says he remembers hurting for Jan in those first days of parenthood because she had to do so many things alone.

As the rehabilitation process continued, Ron began working on a shortened schedule and re-evaluating his life and God's call. He joined our church staff in the fall of 1988 and began attending seminary part-time. Today he is an ordained minister to married adults and a valuable member of our staff. If you had asked him before his accident to describe his life five years down the road, I'm not sure he would have described a single thing the way it is for him and Jan and their family today. Tremendous change has taken place in their lives in every conceivable area, but one thing has remained constant: They have depended on God for all their needs, and even in the midst of pain and tragedy, He has sustained them. They have weathered change because the "changeless core" of Christ is in their lives.

The Chinese term for the word *crisis* is made up of two symbols. One represents despair and the other opportunity. The English word *crisis* is based on the Greek *krinein,* which means "to decide." When we are faced with change (which many of us view as a crisis!), we can choose to view it as a *reason* for failure and despair or as an *opportunity* for growth and creativity. You and I can sit around bemoaning change and longing for "the good old days," or we can get up, move out, and cross our own unique "Jordan" confident that one thing will never change:

When we are faced with change we can choose to view it as a reason for failure and despair or as an opportunity for growth and creativity.

> For I am persuaded that neither death nor life, nor angels nor principalities nor powers, nor things present nor things to come, nor height nor depth, nor any other created thing, shall be able to separate us from the love of God which is in Christ Jesus our Lord.
>
> Romans 8:38–39

Change

- Change is one of the inevitabilities of life. We can count on things to change, and we will never be able to keep them from doing so.
- There is risk in change. Trying something new or doing something the way it's never been done before presents risks, but striving to maintain the status quo may be riskier and more costly in the end.
- Change can be painful, but we experience great growth as we embrace and work through the painful changes of life.
- While the entire universe around us is constantly changing, God will always remain the same. He is immutable—He does not vary with time or circumstance.
- Our response to the challenge of change is critical. We can view change as a threat and put up resistance, resign, or remove ourselves, or we can rescript the negative implications of change and see it as an opportunity for growth. The choice is ours.

Chapter 7

Gold Stallions and Red Lizards

Dealing with Sexual Temptation

And it came to pass after these things that his master's wife cast longing eyes on Joseph, and she said, "Lie with me." But he refused and said to his master's wife, "Look, my master does not know what is with me in the house, and he has committed all that he has to my hand. There is no one greater in this house than I, nor has he kept back anything from me but you, because you are his wife.

How then can I do this great wickedness, and sin against God?" So it was, as she spoke to Joseph day by day, that he did not heed her, to lie with her or to be with her.

Genesis 39:7–10

Gold Stallions and Red Lizards

C. S. Lewis spins a remarkable story in *The Great Divorce* about a little red lizard that a certain ghost carries on his shoulder. The lizard twitches its tail and whispers continually to the ghost, who urges him all the while to be quiet. When a bright and shining presence appears and offers to rid the ghost of his troublesome "baggage," the ghost refuses. He understands that to quiet the beast it is necessary to kill it.

Then a series of rationalizations begins. Perhaps the lizard need not die but can instead be trained, suppressed, put to sleep, or gotten rid of gradually. The presence responds that the gradual approach is useless in dealing with such beasts—it must be all or nothing. Finally, with the ghost's permission, the presence twists the lizard away from him, breaking its back as he flings it to the ground. Then an amazing thing happens. The ghost becomes a perfect man, and at the same moment the lizard becomes an incredibly beautiful silver and gold stallion, full of beauty and power. Then the man leaps astride the great horse, and they ride into the morning as one.

Lewis ends his story with these words: "What is a lizard compared with a stallion? Lust is a poor, weak, whimpering, whispering thing compared with that richness and energy of desire which will arise when lust has been killed."

We live in a world reluctant to part with the little red lizard of lust. The National Center for Health Statistics reports that Americans are becoming sexually active at an earlier age than in past generations. In fact a recent study indicated that over one-fourth of all fifteen-year-old girls are sexually active, and the number increases to 81 percent among nineteen-year-old girls. Nearly three-fourths of all boys are sexually active at seventeen, and 88 percent are at age nineteen.

The consequences? More than 1.5 million abortions were performed in the United States in 1989. Thirty-eight different sexually transmitted diseases are currently at epidemic levels in our country, with three million adolescents contracting such diseases each year. (A record number of 44,000 cases of syphilis was reported in 1989—an increase of 62 percent in three years!) A new strain of gonorrhea has been detected that is completely resistant to all known antibiotics. Of course all these reports have become completely overshadowed by the seriousness of the AIDS epidemic. This disease has become the seventh leading cause of death among fifteen- to twenty-four-year-olds in the U.S., according to a recent report in the journal *Medical Clinics of North America*. (While teenagers comprise only 1.2 percent of total AIDS cases, their number doubles every fourteen months.)

In light of these sobering facts, experts are beginning to discuss some "new" ideas that actually have been around for a very long time. They are abstinence, monogamy, and responsibility. For many years anthropologist Margaret Mead advocated the practice of "serial monogamy"—moving from one monogamous (but temporary) relationship to the next. Today sex researcher Helen Singer Kaplan proposes an alternative to serial or extra-marital relationships that she refers to as "hot monogamy," a term she uses to mean simply working to maintain passion and fidelity in long-term relationships rather than seeking sexual satisfaction outside of them.

Sexual Temptations

Regardless of the trends, sexual temptations have always been with us, and they are here to stay. In Homer's epic poem *The Odyssey,* the sirens were mythical, evil creatures, half-bird and half-woman, who lived on an island surrounded by submerged, jagged rocks. As ships approached the island, the sirens would sing beautiful, seductive songs, luring the sailors to their deaths. When Odysseus' ship approached the island, he ordered the crew to fill their ears with wax to escape the lure of the sirens' songs. This done, he commanded them to bind him to the mast as they passed the island so that he could not change his orders. On another occasion, when the ship of Orpheus sailed by, Orpheus sang a song of his own that was so beautiful and divine that his sailors did not even listen to the sirens' music!

The destructive songs of the sirens can be overcome, but they seldom just stop playing. Potiphar's wife sang one to Joseph as he served daily in his master's household. And we still hear their strains today—in the home, in schools, on the streets, and in the workplace. The lyrics are compellingly simple, much like the ones Joseph heard: "Lie with me." Resisting may seem impossible in our sex-saturated society, but singing along can have disastrous results that carry over to the generations to come.

Joseph came to live in Potiphar's house at a critical time. He was a young man making the transition from favorite son of a wealthy Israelite to favored slave of a powerful Egyptian. He was faced with learning a new language, a new culture, and a new lifestyle. His friends and family were far away, and many of them mistakenly believed that he was dead! Evidently he made the adjustment quite well for he became Potiphar's "right hand man," with charge over every aspect of his master's personal and professional affairs. In Genesis

*S*exual temptations have always been with us, and they are here to stay.

39:2 we learn the secret of his success: "The LORD was with Joseph, and he was a successful man."

Too often the success of an individual is measured by his station in life, but true success is found only by being in the will of God. Any person who is considered successful in a material sense needs to remember that God allowed his success. Joseph discovered a corollary to this truth: Those whom God greatly blesses are always severely tempted by His adversary, Satan. And one of Satan's well-worn ploys (why stop using something when it still works?) is sexual temptation.

The moral climate of Egypt in Potiphar's day set the stage for Joseph's temptation. Art and literature of this period of Egyptian culture were excessively explicit and suggestive. Archaeological findings suggest that immorality was even more pervasive then than it is today! Egypt was the most liberal nation on earth. And Joseph was a lonely man, a long way from home.

Joseph thought living in Potiphar's house was very lonely, but he wasn't the only one. Being a man with a healthy appreciation for beauty, Joseph noticed Potiphar's wife immediately. Since Potiphar spent most of his time away from home, his wife was often alone in the house with Joseph.

But why did she want Joseph? Maybe in all the lavish opulence of her lifestyle she found his simplicity intriguing. Maybe Potiphar never talked to her. Maybe she was just spoiled and couldn't stand the thought of seeing something she couldn't have.

*T*oo often the success of an individual is measured by his station in life, but true success is found only by being in the will of God.

She watched him all the time. And even though the house was quite large, they always seemed to end up in the same room. She may have hinted, but he never acknowledged that he understood the innuendos. Finally she put her case into words he could not ignore. There was no mistaking her meaning when she said, "Lie with me."

Of course Joseph refused. It was unthinkable, really. Potiphar's trust would have been reason enough, but Joseph knew that to lie with her was a great evil and a sin against God. It was then that he discovered she was as persistent as she was beautiful. Day after day, week after week, month after month, the litany was the same: "Lie with me."

Add to his youth and loneliness at this time in his life the fact that Joseph was an extremely attractive young man, "handsome in form and appearance," and you have the makings of a moral disaster. Yet the Bible records that nothing illicit occurred.

Temptations Can Be Resisted

What happened in Joseph's moment of temptation? One day as he was working inside and no other servants were present, Mrs. Potiphar caught him by his coat and demanded again that he take her. He ran. He had no other choice. What was he to do? Try to explain to her that they were two reasonable people who wanted what was right? They weren't, at least not both of them. So he just fled.

If her actions were any indication, *no* was a word she didn't hear often. She was so indignant, she called the other servants and showed them Joseph's coat as evidence of his improper advances toward her! Her concocted story of attempted rape pleased her so much when she told it to the servants, she tried it on Potiphar as well when he returned home.

He probably didn't believe her. But it was easier to deal with an erring servant than a lying wife—and he was a man who valued expediency. By all rights he should have had Joseph killed, and the fact that he did not indicates he suspected her deceit. Nevertheless Joseph left his household that day and was taken to the jail where the king's prisoners were confined—a place Joseph would become quite familiar with in the days to come.

A careful look at Joseph's response to Mrs. Potiphar suggests three reasons why he chose purity over promiscuity in spite of compelling circumstances: "Look, my master does not know what is with me in the house, and he has committed all that he has to my hand. There is no one greater in this house than I, nor has he kept back anything from me but you, because you are his wife. How then can I do this great wickedness, and sin against God?" (Gen. 39:8–9).

The first reason Joseph gave in refusing to commit adultery is *trust*. Potiphar trusted his young aide, and Joseph honored that gift of trust. Some would argue that the trust Joseph sought to uphold was nothing more than a license to take what was offered, but he did not see it that way. In fact many men and women today would view a similar "opportunity" to sin as a way to move up the ladder of life. Not Joseph. Being trusted called out his best.

A young woman in our church shared with me that she never had a set curfew when growing up. Instead her parents asked her before each date or event what time she planned to be home and expected her to keep her word. (I'm certain that had her answer been unreasonable further discussion would have ensued.) While this might not be the best choice for some teenagers, it was for her. She delighted in her parents' trust so much that she routinely came in earlier than they would have required had they set the hour. Because they trusted her to make wise choices, she tried to honor them by consistently doing so. It never occurred to her to jeopardize the gift of trust she'd earned and enjoyed by abusing it.

The second reason given in Joseph's refusal of Mrs. Potiphar's advances was simply that she was off limits. Isn't it interesting that the same rationale Joseph used against the opportunity to sin, Eve used as an excuse for sin? While what was off limits attracted Eve, it repelled Joseph. Tell a child no and watch his response. Almost like magic the thing that has been denied becomes the most attractive thing in his world. What is excusable in a child, say, crying for a candy bar or even sneaking one when a parent looks away, is not responsible behavior in an adult. Ingratitude and selfishness are at the heart of every act of disobedience. Joseph understood at an early age that *no* meant "no," and he didn't waste his life wishing for what was declared off limits to him.

The final reasons given in Joseph's refusal of Mrs. Potiphar was simply that to lie with her would be to *sin against God*. Christian physician John White coined the term "new adulterers" in his excellent book *Eros Defiled*. He says the new adulterers are identified by their attempts to justify or re-name what is in fact sin:

> To begin with they contemptuously toss the ancient rules into the garbage can. Their arrogance offends me. What matter that people have for centuries tested and proved their worth! Rules that may have been relevant in earlier, less complex cultures are inappropriate in our sophisticated age. They will cooly tell me, "Yes, we did go to bed together. That's how we felt about it, and we see no point concealing it. I have to be true to myself. I want to be me."[1]

No matter what we choose to call it, sin is sin, and God is not confused about it, although too often we are. We can argue that we are simply expressing our natural desires or being totally honest about our feelings, but until we admit that what we are doing really is sinning against a holy God, we are misguided at best and willfully disobedient at worst.

No matter what we choose to call it, sin is sin, and God is not confused about it.

We live in a moral universe, whether we choose to recognize that fact or not. Four hundred years before the law that reads "You shall not commit adultery" was given to Moses on Mount Sinai, Joseph understood that sleeping with another man's wife is not only wrong, it is an affront to God's standard of holiness. God was more real to Joseph than anything else in his life, and it was this undeniable reality that enabled him to live a life of sexual purity.

No Place to Hide

Some years back when I was pastoring a church in South Carolina, a college sophomore named Bill dropped by my office to talk. He was clearly troubled about something, and when I asked him what was wrong, he simply said, "I can't find God anymore." I asked Bill when he'd last felt God's presence, and he haltingly began a story I've heard more times than I can count. The details change of course but little else ever does.

At nineteen Bill was a virgin, a condition most of his college friends looked upon as a character flaw. After a lot of teasing and the constant pressure of his peers to change that fact, he took a consenting co-ed to a hotel room near the university and had sex with her. As he was telling his story, Bill looked like anything but a young man who had solved a problem. At the time, however, he thought his plan was bullet-proof. The girl was willing. The hotel room was private and anonymous. No one would see. No one would know. But Bill believed that room was the place where he and God parted company, and he insisted he had not been able to find God since.

I opened my Bible to Psalm 139, handed it to Bill, and asked him to read out loud David's words on the omnipresence of God:

> O LORD, You have searched me and known me.
>
> You know my sitting down and my rising up;
>
> You understand my thought afar off.
>
> You comprehend my path and my lying down,
>
> And are acquainted with all my ways.
>
> For there is not a word on my tongue,
>
> But behold, O LORD, You know it altogether.
>
> You have hedged me behind and before,

And laid Your hand upon me.

Such knowledge is too wonderful for me;

It is high, I cannot attain it.

Where can I go from Your Spirit?

Or where can I flee from Your presence?

If I ascend to heaven, You are there;

If I make my bed in hell, behold, You are there.

If I take the wings of the morning,

And dwell in the uttermost parts of the sea,

Even there Your hand shall lead me,

And Your right hand shall hold me.

Psalm 139:1–10

As we read, Bill discovered this truth: His problem was not that he couldn't find God, but that he couldn't get away from Him, not even in a cheap hotel room. Sin makes us want to hide from God, but everywhere we run we find that He is already there. There's just no place we can go to get away from Him. If God is real to you and me, we can't lose Him, no matter where we go or what we do. He is "the hound of heaven"—and He never hides. But we often run from Him!

God never left Bill, and He never left Joseph. The reasons for Joseph's refusal to commit adultery might have come to naught except for one thing. He did more than think about them; he acted on them! Mrs. Potiphar was a persistent woman (most temptations are more than "fleeting"), and she pleaded with Joseph—day after day, week after week, perhaps even for months and years. We can guess that there was more involved than mere words. Like the sirens her seductive music was woven of sight and sound and embellished with engaging innuendo. The difficult situation reached its point of crisis when she seized him one day and took his robe in her hand! Joseph's manly response? He ran! The literal translation of the Hebrew says, "Joseph ran out into the streets." There is only one appropriate response to

*T*here is only one appropriate response to the bombardment of sexual temptation: RUN!

the bombardment of sexual temptation: RUN! He knew better than to attempt to talk things out, to reason, or to debate the issue. It would have been useless to say, "Let's discuss this like two mature adults," especially when only one mature adult was present! When we are faced with temptation of this nature, there is no better choice than the one Joseph made. Flee!

Affair-proof Your Marriage

*W*hile there may be a point-of-no-return in matters of sexual temptation, there is often much we can do to avoid reaching that point.

Sometimes the circumstances surrounding our temptations are those of our own design. While there may be a point-of-no-return in matters of sexual temptation, there is often much we can do to avoid reaching that point. Many excellent books have been written on this subject; one of the best is *The Myth of the Greener Grass* by J. Alan Petersen.

If, considering all the self-help courses available to us today, I could add one course that I believe would greatly benefit anyone—married, divorced, or never married—I would propose a course entitled "How to Affair-proof Your Marriage." Even if you never needed it the odds are overwhelming that you would know at least one person who would. Before we ever reach the "flee" stage, there is much we can do to establish the groundwork for marital fidelity. For instance . . .

Refuse to be put in compromising situations

If you are married, take care in choosing your most intimate friends. Pay specific attention to friendships with other married couples. This warning may seem unnecessary until we consider the familiarity of the refrain, "He ran off with his wife's best friend." So many affairs begin this way that we're seldom shocked any longer to hear the words. Don't be caught in friendship traps. Remember how Wile E. Coyote in those old cartoons got caught in every trap he set for the Roadrunner? We'd laugh and shake our heads at his schemes, knowing that before long he'd be in the ditch or under the rock or at the bottom of a gulch he'd meant for the Roadrunner. Some of the funniest cartoons are all-too-sad caricatures of real life.

Seemingly innocent friendships can so quickly become traps that we don't even recognize the danger. How do we avoid them? First of all make sure your most intimate friends are genuine Christians who have deep, meaningful, growing marriages. Do not discuss your marriage or theirs unless it's woman-to-woman or man-to-man. If you are a woman and the other man asks to talk to you concerning problems in his marriage, make it clear that your husband will be included in the conversation. The same principle holds true for a man.

Be aware of the special temptations of the business world

I read recently of a lunchtime conversation among thirteen professional women, eleven married and two unmarried. One of the unmarried women, who was seeing someone seriously and contemplating marriage, asked the others how many of them had been completely faithful to their spouses and had never had an affair. Only one of the married women indicated that she had been totally faithful!

The workplace is the setting in which we normally spend half our waking hours, and it is a place of tremendous tension, challenge, frustration, and vulnerability. With over half of married women working today, the corporate world is no longer a man's domain. And people in similar circumstances with similar concerns and pressures will naturally be drawn together in comaraderie and mutual support. Just recognizing this fact can somewhat diffuse the inherent danger. I know one married man who says he has made it his personal policy to never go out to eat alone with any woman from his office. His decision was not a matter of appropriateness or acceptable behavior; it was simply a choice not to play to his own weakness, or to someone else's.

Define the boundaries of your relationships with those of the opposite sex

A psychotherapist I know never schedules a woman as his last appointment of the day. It's a hedge he has against temptation. When I have done pastoral counseling, I have established some hedges of my own. (Obstacle courses might be a more accurate description.) I sit behind my desk—and it's a big desk. I place a Bible on top of the desk, next to pictures of my wife, our children, and now my grandchildren. I always begin any counseling time with prayer. There is an open window behind me and a secretary on the other side of the door, who has been asked to come in at the sound of anything out of the ordinary. Do I think these precautions are extreme? They may seem that way; but for anyone who might in a vulnerable moment be a little more interested in the pastor than she should, they are a safeguard.

Some might argue that such firm boundaries discourage any possibility of true friendships between the sexes. And many popular movies these days explore this intriguing possibility. But when C. S. Lewis's *The Four Loves* first appeared over thirty years ago, he contended that it was a rather unlikely prospect at best:

In most societies at most periods friendships will be between men and men or between women and women. The sexes will have met one another in affection and in eros but not in this love. For they will seldom have had with each other the companionship in common activities which is the matrix of friendship.[2]

Lewis hypothesized, however, that friendship would be possible,

where men and women work side by side, or in the mission field, or among authors and artists.... To be sure, what is offered as friendship on one side may be mistaken as eros on the other, with painful and embarrassing results.[3]

Such is the case today. Men and women meet as equals and colleagues each day in the workplace, sharing job responsibilities, common interests, and mutual goals. Warm, genuine friendships between members of the opposite sex are possible, but the guidelines need to be firmly in place.

Paul urges Timothy in 1 Timothy 5:1–2 to consider younger women as he would his sisters and older women as mothers. A wise man or woman will adopt a similar mindset and will put up boundaries at the slightest spark of chemistry between him or her and a member of the opposite sex. (If you don't know what I mean by *chemistry*, I'm not sure you have the good sense to get out of your driveway in the morning!)

Warm, genuine friendships between members of the opposite sex are possible, but the guidelines need to be firmly in place.

Be your mate's host or hostess

*I*magine how our marriages would change if we sought to be a host or hostess to our spouses in our own homes!

Most of us would agree that children have no business getting married, and yet it happens all the time. In fact any time two adults marry, there are two children involved as well, because we all have childish ways within us. Part of being a child is behaving like a guest in your own home. If you don't agree, just remember the surprise of moving away from home for the first time and discovering that the laundry doesn't automatically get washed, folded, and put away! If a man or woman enters marriage and assumes the role of guest, the relationship is in for a bad time! If a marriage can on occasion weather one guest, it can seldom withstand two.

My wife surprised me one evening by suggesting that we spend the night in the guest room. She explained that by doing so we would be able to anticipate the needs of some overnight guests who would be arriving soon. If a light bulb needed changing, we would know. If the alarm clock was sitting more than an arm's length from the bed, we could move it closer. If there were not enough towels in the guest bathroom, we would discover that and remedy the problem before our guests arrived. Pretty considerate, wasn't it? Imagine how our marriages would change if we sought to be a host or hostess to our spouses in our own homes! A good host or hostess is primarily concerned with meeting the needs of his or her guests and not with having personal needs met first.

Dr. Willard Harley, a Massachusetts psychologist, surveyed the basic needs of men and women in marriage and found (this is amazing) that the needs are completely different. According to Dr. Harley's survey, the top five basic needs of the female in marriage are:[4]

1. Affection
2. Communication
3. Openness/Honesty
4. Financial Support
5. Family Commitment

The male's top five basic needs are:

1. Sexual Fulfillment
2. Recreational Companionship
3. An Attractive Wife
4. Domestic Support
5. Admiration

Looking at both lists, it becomes obvious that if we give our spouses what we need, hoping to receive the same in return, we will miss the mark every time. Therefore, instead of giving what *we* need, we must affair-proof our marriages by striving to give what our partners need. Incidentally, if the idea of treating a spouse as an honored guest seems offensive, consider Jesus' words as he settled a who's-the-greatest argument between his disciples. The story is recorded in the twenty-second chapter of Luke's Gospel.

> The kings of the Gentiles exercise lordship over
> them, and those who exercise authority over them
> are called "benefactors." But not so among you;
> on the contrary, he who is greatest among you, let
> him be as the younger, and he who governs as he
> who serves. For who is greater, he who sits at the
> table, or he who serves? Is it not he who sits at the
> table? Yet I am among you as the One who serves.
>
> Luke 22:25–27

Remember the promises you made

The primary sin of adultery is not that sexual intercourse has taken place between partners who are not married to each other. Instead it is the breaking of a covenant. In adulterous relationships promises are broken, and men and women cheat each other and steal what does not belong to them. When you stood at the altar with your mate and before God said the words *I do*, you made a marriage covenant with your mate *and with God*. When you have sexual intercourse with someone to whom you are not married, you break that covenant. If you are a Christian, not only do you defraud your mate, you unite the Lord Jesus Christ who lives in you with that which blatantly contradicts His plan or purpose.

*I*f you are a Christian, not only do you defraud your mate, you unite the Lord Jesus Christ who lives in you with that which blatantly contradicts His plan or purpose.

The biblical concept of *covenant* involves two distinct parties who bind themselves to each other and, in doing so, make that bond the most significant thing in their lives. Their lives revolve around their covenant the way the planets revolve around the sun. God illustrated this precept by establishing a covenant with His chosen people that would stand in spite of their waywardness. It was not Israel's performance as a nation that guaranteed her a special relationship with Jehovah God, it was His choosing of her and the ratification of that choice by the covenant he made with her. The closeness of that relationship depended upon Israel's and God's attention to the promises they had made to each other and their obedience to those vows. In the same way the health of our marriage relationships is dependent upon the diligence with which we work to maintain our vows.

Dr. Tom McGuiness, a counseling psychologist in New Jersey, gives this explanation of why many affairs take place:

Married people seek out or succumb to affairs when they feel devalued or less than fully alive. They are bored. Overburdened. People who have affairs have a child's deep longing to be touched, caressed, held, hugged and kissed, whether they admit it or not. They want happy surprises. That might mean a sentimental unexpected gift every once in a while. More important, it is the dependable gift of time and caring. The present of shared ideas, experiences, stories, nonsense and games, including sexual games. They want the world to butt out. They want a loving friend, a pal who isn't judgmental. They want someone to convince them they're still loved, lovable and very special. For a little while, now and then, they want out from under the grown-up responsibilities that have become predictable, dreary and difficult.[5]

If these are the reasons extra-marital affairs occur, couldn't we guard against them by seeking to meet our mates' deepest needs for affection, security, friendship, and sexual fulfillment? Maybe the best prevention for an affair outside marriage is to plan one with the man or woman we're married to!

We pay attention to the things that matter to us. If we want to be in good physical shape we try to eat right, exercise, and stretch and tone our muscles. If we want to get ahead in our vocations, we read, we stay abreast of current trends, we study—sometimes we even return to school to learn new methods and practices that will enhance our job performance. But

*M*aybe the best prevention for an affair outside marriage is to plan one with the man or woman we're married to!

somehow we expect our marriages to sizzle while we sit side by side on the couch, glued to the television or absorbed in the newspaper, night after night. Obviously "How to Affair-proof Your Marriage" is a course that requires continual homework.

Joseph's ancient stand for sexual purity against nearly overwhelming odds has tremendous implications for you and me if we are really serious about living "overcoming" lives. If Joseph could withstand the temptations of his culture, there is hope for us as well. The lurking danger of adultery, the increasing acceptance of homosexuality as an acceptable, alternative lifestyle, the alarming increase in reports of child molestation, and the proliferation of pornography are dangerous but not insurmountable. We simply must remember *Whose* we are.

There is an old slave market in Charleston, South Carolina. This historical place stands as a reminder of a time in America when men were sold like animals to the highest bidder. Over a hundred years ago in that very market, a group of slaves were brought in to face their buyers. As the auction began, one of the bidders noticed a slave who stood taller than all the others. The fact that he was unafraid and keen of mind was evident in every move he made. The intrigued bidder nudged his friend. "What's different about that one?" he asked. Another man overheard his question and answered, "Back in Africa, that one was the son of a king, and he has not forgotten it yet."

We too belong to a King, and He has given us the promise of His indwelling presence to combat all that the world can confront us with, including the constant, whispering presence of the little red lizard of lust. Be aware and beware! The red lizard is alive and well.

Sexual Temptation

- Sexual temptation is as old as time and it's here to stay. Lust will not be quieted, compromised, or lulled to sleep—it must be dealt with.

- God says sex outside of the marriage covenant is wrong, because it contradicts the purpose for which He designed it.
- The best defense is a good offense. We can begin to affair-proof our marriages by focusing our attention on our mates and cultivating that bond.
- God is as interested in the sexual choices of His children as He is any other aspect of their lives. He is present, even when the choices we make are poor ones.
- A personal relationship with Jesus Christ and an understanding of His principles concerning our sexuality are the most effective weapons we have to combat sexual temptation in our lives.

Chapter 8

Only the Lonely

Dealing with Loneliness

"But remember me when it is well with you, and please show kindness to me; make mention of me to Pharaoh, and get me out of this house. For indeed I was stolen away from the land of the Hebrews; and also I have done nothing here that they should put me into the dungeon." Yet the chief butler did not remember Joseph, but forgot him.

Genesis 40:14–15, 23

Only the Lonely

An elderly woman sits in a nursing home, watching through the front window for the sight of a familiar car. She remembers the promises of children and grandchildren who said they would come again soon. Each morning she gets up, brushes her hair, arranges the pictures in her room, and puts on a fresh dress in hopes that today will be the day. She is waiting.

A college student stares at the phone in the box-like dormitory room he shares with a near stranger. He had close friends at home, good friends, who had chosen nearby colleges. But he had accepted a scholarship at an excellent school in another state. He wishes someone would call . . . sometime. He is homesick.

A middle-aged man sits alone at a kitchen table, waiting for the coffee to brew. He has made three cups. He used to make six, but he is a widower now and learning to live with new proportions. Everything in the kitchen seems to remind him of his wife. He is trying to adjust, to be grateful for the good years, but he misses her.

This is the third baby shower she has been to this year, and it is only April. She is thirty-four, and more than anything would like to have a husband and a child. She is thankful for the things her career has afforded her and all the activity that never seems to stop. Yet each night before she falls asleep, she asks God one more time for that which she wants so desperately, a family and a home. She continues to pray and to hope.

There's no escaping loneliness. Young or old, married or single, we all face times of loneliness.

*Y*oung or old, married or single, we all face times of loneliness.

Joseph knew loneliness first-hand in the years that followed his unjust imprisonment for the alleged assault of Potiphar's wife.

Even in jail, potentially one of the loneliest places on earth, God was with Joseph. The chief jailer trusted him as Potiphar had, and Joseph had not been in jail long when he was put in charge of all the other prisoners. Isn't it strange? As a slave he was over all the household, and as a prisoner he was over all the jail. It seems that whatever he did God crowned his efforts with success.

Joseph met some very interesting people in jail. Two of them were servants in the king's own household: his butler and his baker. Joseph never knew the details of their offenses, but whatever they had done infuriated Pharaoh, who placed them with Joseph in the captain of the bodyguard's jail. They were all confined together for some time.

One night both men had dreams they did not understand. The next morning when Joseph asked them why they looked sad, they said they'd had dreams, but had no one to interpret them. Joseph remarked that interpretations belong to God, but being something of a dreamer himself, he encouraged them to tell him their dreams.

The interpretation of the butler's dream was a positive one. In three days he would be released from prison and restored to his former office in the service of Pharaoh. The interpretation of the baker's dream was not happy. He would be hanged in three days, and the birds would eat his flesh.

Both events happened just as Joseph predicted. When the butler walked away from the prison, Joseph pleaded with him to remember his interpreter-friend and ask Pharaoh for Joseph's release when the opportunity arose.

The sting of isolation was especially sharp in the years following the release of his fellow prisoner. Once assured of his own freedom the butler promised Joseph that he would remember him and try to obtain his freedom as well, but more than two years went by with no word of a release for Joseph.

I believe those two years were the lowest point of Joseph's life. He was homesick ("for indeed I was stolen away from the land of the Hebrews"), wrongly accused ("and also I have done nothing here that they should put me into the dungeon"), and frustrated ("get me out of this house"). He was isolated; yet he was dependent on others for his existence. Each day he hoped for release, prayed for change. But for two long years nothing about his circumstances changed. He remained shut up in an Egyptian prison, far from home and aching for freedom.

Former White House special assistant and speechwriter Peggy Noonan recognized the modern epidemic of loneliness from her own unique political vantage point. "The biggest problem in America," she says, "the biggest problem in any modern, industrialized society, is loneliness." For this reason she maintains that "a great speech from a leader to the people eases our isolation, breaks down the walls, includes people; it takes them inside a spinning thing and makes them part of the gravity."

At the center of loneliness is a desire to be connected. Reduced to its least common denominator, loneliness is longing to hear a word from someone, to be seen as significant, to be recognized, remembered, affirmed, counted, known. The feeling is not to be confused with aloneness. It is possible to be lonely in a noisy crowd or in a circle of intimate friendship. Sometimes loneliness involves waiting, and waiting is often a solitary thing.

The questions Joseph must have asked during what was undoubtedly the loneliest time of his life echo those posed today by the disappointed, the disenfranchised, the forgotten: Why am I here? Does anyone care? Has God forgotten me? Will He ever act on my behalf?

Why Am I Here?

Many of us operate under the assumption that life's circumstances are determined by our own actions. If things are rosy we assume it's because we've been "good." If not we imagine that our circumstances are the direct result of bad choices or mistakes that we have made. The problem with this perspective is that it makes man the center of his own universe, and he is not. The apostle Paul blasts the Colossian Christians out of this kind of egocentric thinking by pointing them instead to the Son of God:

*A*t the center of loneliness is a desire to be connected.

> For by Him all things were created that are in
> heaven and that are on earth, visible and invisible,
> whether thrones or dominions or principalities or
> powers. All things were created through Him and
> for Him. And He is before all things, and in Him
> all things consist.
>
> Colossians 1:16–17

A God-centered worldview like this rarely accompanies loneliness, but a self-centered view invites it!

*A*sking why is seldom fruitful, but acceptance almost always is.

Joseph resisted the tendency to see his unpleasant situation solely as the result of his own actions. In fact he did just the opposite. He stated that he had done nothing to land himself in prison. He refused to see his present difficulty as a sentence stemming from past sins. (While we do at times face the inevitable consequences of our own sin, an honest "gut check" can usually tell us if we are to blame.) Job, another Old Testament character, also steadfastly (and correctly) maintained his innocence in relation to the multitude of calamities he faced. Only a humble man can say, "I am not the cause of everything."

"It's all my fault" thinking is not restricted to ancient cultures. I know of single adults today who are convinced that God is withholding marriage from them because of an immoral past. There are widows and widowers who believe God took their mates because they were not the loving, kind, godly spouses they should have been. Many in financial difficulty assume that they are being punished for mishandling money in the past, and others view illness as God's retribution for a multitude of sins, both real and imagined.

The truth is that no matter what we do, lonely times—periods of confusion, uncertainty, and heartbreak—will come. Asking why is seldom fruitful, although it's a perfectly human response. But *acceptance* almost always is. It was true that Joseph was unjustly imprisoned. It was true that the butler had forgotten him. It was true that the world seemed to be passing by this godly, gifted young man. But he accepted every trying circumstance and continued to wait expectantly for the day when life would change again, when the dreams God had given him as a young boy would begin to come true.

Does Anyone Care?

Last Christmas our church family did something we had never done before. We developed a program called "Angels of Mercy" as a gift to those in our city who were experiencing hard times. For several weeks prior to the holidays we collected clothing, shoes, and toys to distribute to families who were spending Christmas in shelters around our city or who were simply in need and unable to provide for themselves.

The response was tremendous. We had literally a warehouse full of clothing for men, women, and children of all ages and sizes, and our worship center began to look like Toys R Us as an incredible collection of gifts accumulated week by week. Thousands of church members were involved in this effort, and when the collecting was done, our "guests" were brought by bus to our campus, fed a special holiday dinner (generously provided each night by a local restaurant owner), entertained with music of the season, given the gospel message, and "gifted" with bags of clothing and toys that matched (as closely as we could manage) the wish lists they had filled out on the bus ride over.

The individual stories that came out of this effort were truly amazing. One busload of guests were Vietnamese people who had been in America only a few days and spoke almost no English. I'm certain they did not understand the words of greeting that were spoken or the Christmas carols that were sung. But by the time the evening was over and they got back on the bus to return to the shelter, their faces affirmed an understanding of one sure thing—someone in this strange new place cared about them. Someone cared.

*O*ne of the
most
troublesome
symptoms of
loneliness is
the feeling
that we
suffer or
celebrate in
isolation,
that no one
understands
and no one
cares.

*T*he turning
point in
Joseph's
dungeon
experience
came when
he ceased to
wait
anxiously on
the butler
and began to
wait
expectantly
on God.

Knowing that someone cares about us satisfies a deep hunger in you and me. One of the most troublesome symptoms of loneliness is the feeling that we suffer or celebrate in isolation, that no one understands and no one cares. I am certain that for every family we shared Christmas with last year there were hundreds who never knew that someone cared about their unique predicament. I am equally certain that the pews of our nation's churches contain countless people who feel utterly alone in their circumstances. How many nights did Joseph fall asleep in prison wondering if the butler cared that he was still behind bars?

Has God Forgotten Me?

Sometimes the world forgets us. Sometimes it really does seem that no one cares. But nothing I can think of is more isolating or frightening than the belief that God Himself has forgotten us. It is one of the Enemy's favorite lies.

God knows where we are! For the elderly woman in the nursing home, the homesick college student, the single adult longing for marriage, the widow or widower aching with loss, the good news is that God knows. There is no situation that removes us from His understanding, watchful eye.

I believe the turning point in Joseph's dungeon experience came when he ceased to wait anxiously on the butler and began to wait expectantly on God. For many days after the butler left, Joseph was filled with a new hope. He whistled. He sang. He imagined what he would do when news of his release came. But the days stretched into months and the months into years, and there was no word from the butler. Could he have forgotten? What if he did not believe Joseph's innocence? Could Potiphar have persuaded Pharaoh never to release Joseph? There was no way for him to know, and he had never been more lonely in his life.

Each day was very much like the day before, and slowly his hope in the butler's advocacy dwindled. But when it did another hope began to take its place. Joseph began to hope in God again. After all He had been the one who transformed all the other "tragedies" of his life into triumphs. If he was ever to be released he was certain his release would come from Him. And if not, whatever good might come of his imprisonment would come from Him as well.

So in the loneliness of a prison cell Joseph learned a mighty lesson in waiting on the God who is never late. But it was a struggle, and he counted those "silent" years as some of the darkest of his life.

The world may have forgotten him, but he was certain that God remembered. He might spend the rest of his life in prison, but God knew his whereabouts, and God would make something beautiful of his life.

Our high school and junior high students have a song that's become a standard on our summer beach retreats. It's called "Something Beautiful," and its message encourages me when circumstances seem to deny God's presence:

> Something beautiful, something good,
> All my confusion He understood.
> All I had to offer Him was brokenness and strife,
> But He made something beautiful of my life.[1]

Joseph knew that God had already begun making "something beautiful" out of his life, and he never wavered in the assurance that God would complete what He had begun.

Will God Ever Act on My Behalf?

It's one thing to believe that God *knows* our circumstances. It's another thing entirely to believe that He will act on our behalf. The first involves faith in who He is. The second requires hope in what He will do. Poet Emily Dickinson said hope "is the thing with feathers / that perches in the soul / that sings the tune without the words / and never stops at all."[2] The apostle Paul wrote of the hope of the glory of God:

> We also glory in tribulations, knowing that tribu-
> lation produces perseverance; and perseverance,
> character; and character, hope. Now hope does not
> disappoint, because the love of God has been
> poured out in our hearts.
>
> Romans 5:3–5

*H*ope in God is a choice that will not disappoint! It is an absolutely reasonable choice no matter what our circumstances, because it is based on faith in who He is.

Hope in God is a choice that will not disappoint! It is an absolutely reasonable choice no matter what our circumstances, because it is based on faith in who He is. Because He is righteous and holy, His actions will always be an expression of His character. There is an acronym used in the computer industry that is easy to spell and hard to say: WYSIWYG. It simply means "what you see is what you get." Just so with God. He is not capricious or arbitrary; He is faithful and true. He will not act in ways that contradict His character.

Joseph's belief that God would continue to act on his behalf was based on his experiential knowledge of God. He knew that God had spared him from death at the hands of his brothers. He knew God had placed him in a position of respect in Potiphar's household. He had seen God's hand in his life beginning with his childhood dreams, and he trusted that the same care would continue. It was just a matter of time.

You may be thinking, "Well, God has never acted on my behalf before. Why should I expect Him to start now?" But He *has* acted on your behalf and mine in a life-changing way:

> For when we were still without strength, in due
> time Christ died for the ungodly. For scarcely for
> a righteous man will one die; yet perhaps for a
> good man someone would even dare to die. But
> God demonstrates His own love toward us, in that
> while we were still sinners, Christ died for us.
>
> Romans 5:6–8

The faithfulness in question is not His—it is ours! Will we wait expectantly and continue to trust Him even if we hurt? Even if we are lonely? Even if we are in pain? Will we continue to take our needs to Him in prayer even when He is silent? Charles Spurgeon suggests that the answer to the long-suffering, seeking prayer may be the richest blessing of all:

> Remember, the longer the blessing is in coming,
> the richer it will be when it arrives. That which is
> gained speedily by a single prayer is sometimes
> only a second rate blessing; but that which is
> gained after many a desperate tug and many an
> awful struggle, is a full weighted and precious
> blessing. That which costs us the most prayer will
> be worth the most.[3]

The Loneliness of Waiting

Molly Remkus is one of the newest faces in our nursery. All babies are special of course, but to appreciate how Molly's arrival ministered to our church family I need to tell you first about her parents. Craig and Wendi Remkus met in our single adult department and after a lengthy courtship, were married. Both had demanding careers at the start of their marriage, but this young couple knew from the beginning of their life together that having a family would be their first priority.

When Craig and Wendi decided the time was right to start their family, they faced what thousands of other couples today are confronted with: the pain of infertility. For several years this fine young couple struggled with their desire for a child, and continued to hope and pray. Wendi underwent various medical procedures and eventually retired to devote all her energies to the child they were praying for.

As the likelihood of giving birth to a child diminished Craig and Wendi began to investigate adoption. They learned that the adoption process is complicated, expensive, and worst of all, slow. But they began to pursue interviews with two separate agencies in hope that they would be accepted, and as the interviews and paperwork proceeded, they continued to pray along with their family and friends.

Craig and Wendi were accepted as candidates by both agencies. When one agency offered greater hope than the other, they prayed and withdrew their application from the second agency, believing it would give other couples in the same position a better opportunity as well. They were visited by a case worker in their home and told that an office interview would likely follow in a few months. Through every step of the process, they continued to pray for their baby.

A short time after their home interview a representative of the agency called and asked if Craig and Wendi could come in for their office interview in a few days. They agreed and drove to the city where the office was located. (The reason they were called so soon after their initial interview was unknown to them at the time, but I'll tell you so you can follow the story as it unfolds. The caseworker for the young woman who was Molly's biological mother dreamed about the Remkuses as potential adoptive parents for Molly and then requested that her supervisor include their file for the mother to review, even though their second interview was not yet scheduled. The supervisor agreed and scheduled the interview as soon as possible.)

Before the interview took place, the birthmother reviewed the files on the potential adoptive parents with her caseworker. The maternal grandmother of the child was a Christian and wanted very much for the baby to be adopted into a Christian home. Craig and Wendi were the only Christians among the parents presented to this mother and daughter. As they learned more about Craig and Wendi, they chose them to be the baby's parents, even before the office interview was held.

As they look back Craig and Wendi can remember that a few things about the interview seemed odd. The hallway outside was bustling with activity, a woman carrying a car seat kept walking by the door and looking in. But the moment they remember most vividly is the moment the caseworker said, "You've been accepted as adoptive parents, and *your daughter is waiting outside.*"

I don't know a lot about adoption, but I'm told that the chances of the story you've just read taking place are a million to one. But it happened. And Craig and Wendi will tell you that Molly Remkus is God's provision and His blessed answer to all their prayers and tears.

Couples who struggle with infertility tell me that the experience is incredibly isolating. Childlessness is one of life's lonely places. The Remkuses would tell you that it taught them the importance of giving God everything—every dream, every longing, every hope, every fear. Trusting God with their desire for a child and giving that desire to Him was the key to surviving the struggle.

What Can We Do with the Hurt?

Oblation is an old-fashioned word. It means the act of offering something up in worship or devotion to God. The hurts we experience in life seldom seem useful at the time, but they make excellent material for sacrifice. We can offer our feelings of loneliness, sadness, uncertainty, doubt, fear, and suffering *in oblation* to God. He will receive them, and as with the impossibly meager loaves and fish of a peasant boy, He will just as surely bless and use them for our good and His glory.

As Joseph waited on God in the darkness of a dungeon, I believe he learned this secret. Instead of being a curse, his loneliness became a gift that he could give to the One who knew his circumstance and was able to deliver him. Elisabeth Elliot (twice widowed and now married for a third time) was once asked to speak on the trials of widowhood. She refused, saying that she did not view either of her experiences as a trial but rather a gift from God given for a particular time.

> *T*he hurts we experience in life seldom seem useful at the time, but they make excellent material for sacrifice.

Are you lonely? Are there circumstances in your life you are praying that God will change? Can you identify with Joseph's dungeon days? Accept the place where you are right now. Maybe you are single and want to be married. Perhaps you are married and longing for a child or separated and praying for reconciliation. Whatever your situation try to thank God for it, even if it doesn't make sense to you. Understand that while people may forget us, God never does. He has begun and will continue to act on our behalf.

Loneliness

- Lonely people tend to overfocus on themselves. A heart steadfastly focused on God is seldom lonely.
- Acceptance is the first step to making a situation tolerable. Asking *why* is seldom a productive choice.
- The world may forget us, but God never will. He knows our circumstances, and He cares deeply about our needs.
- Our perspective changes when we cease to wait on our circumstances to change and begin to wait on God to reveal Himself in them.

Chapter 9

Trumped!

How to Handle
Success Successfully

*And Pharaoh said to Joseph, "See, I have set
you over all the land of Egypt." Then Pharaoh took his signet ring off his hand and put
it on Joseph's hand; and he clothed him in
garments of fine linen and put a gold chain
around his neck. And he had him ride in the
second chariot which he had; and they cried
out before him, "Bow the knee!" So he set him
over all the land of Egypt.*

Genesis 41:41–43

Trumped! How to Handle Success Successfully

An underlying truth is beginning to emerge as we explore the life of Joseph: In every circumstance or trial he faced, God was even more real to Joseph than the trial itself. His unusual family situation would probably not be considered healthy today, but God fed Joseph's spirit with dreams that encouraged and inspired him. His earthly father's passivity was graciously counterbalanced by a Heavenly Father who was actively and intimately involved in his daily affairs.

In spite of the lack of discipline in his home, Joseph had learned from His Heavenly Father a self-discipline that equipped him with a well-honed sense of right and wrong. When life put him "in the pit," he was sustained by a steady hope that kept him faithful regardless of his surroundings. Neither adversity nor temptation could defeat him. Potiphar's wife was no match for Joseph's strong moral stand and his determination to remain faithful, first to his God and second to his benefactor, Potiphar himself.

In every circumstance or trial he faced, God was even more real to Joseph than the trial itself.

In every difficult circumstance Joseph prospered, because God was with him. But his toughest test did not come through adversity. Instead it arrived "dressed to the nines" in unbelievable prosperity. To keep God real in times of exaltation and success is one of life's most difficult challenges.

Joseph the dreamer was finally released from prison to interpret one of Pharaoh's dreams. He had dreamt of seven healthy cows followed by seven gaunt cows walking out of the Nile River. He had also dreamt of seven healthy ears of grain being swallowed by seven scraggly ones. Pharoah had consulted his court magicians and wise men, but found no one who could explain his dreams. The butler, who had been free for two years, finally remembered Joseph and recommended that Pharoah send for him.

God told Joseph exactly what the dreams meant. The two dreams were one and the same. The lean cows and the bad ears meant that seven years of famine would follow the seven years of plenty. And the fact that the dream was repeated meant that God would quickly bring it to pass. God gave him the precise interpretation that would both establish Joseph's credibility and ensure not just his freedom, but his rise to the top as well.

Joseph's counsel that a wise overseer was needed to guide the land through the imminent times of famine and hardship prompted Pharaoh to turn to Joseph himself for such leadership.

Was Joseph surprised? Yes, but he shouldn't have been. All his life God had placed him in the most unlikely positions of authority, and this was just one more example of His provision. Pharaoh announced to all who could hear that Joseph was to be his righthand man, and that Joseph's word would be law throughout the land. Only on the throne would Pharoah be greater than Joseph.

In John 14:17 Jesus describes the Helper God provides who has the qualities that Pharaoh saw in Joseph: "the Spirit of truth, whom the world cannot receive, because it neither sees Him nor knows Him." While Pharaoh could not describe it this way, he saw in Joseph exactly the kind of man Egypt needed for the days ahead:

Then Pharaoh said to Joseph, "Inasmuch as God has shown you all this, there is no one as discerning and wise as you. You shall be over my house, and all my people shall be ruled according to your word; only in regard to the throne will I be greater than you."

Genesis 41:39–40

*S*urviving prosperity with our values intact is indeed a learned skill that must be carefully developed.

Even the special treatment afforded him as Jacob's favorite son did not compare to the splendor and power of life as Egypt's "prime minister." Pharaoh gave Joseph a new name and one of his daughters for a wife. Joseph wanted for nothing. He controlled everything—everything—in the most powerful nation on earth. And he was barely thirty years old.

Adversity tests our mettle, and oftentimes it brings out the best in us, calling up resources we may never have realized we possessed. Prosperity tests us, too, but in a different way. Success, especially at a young age, can bring out the worst in us and display character flaws that the fires of adversity never reveal. No wonder the apostle Paul wrote to the Philippians about the value of finding contentment regardless of circumstances:

I know how to get along with humble means, and I also know how to live in prosperity; in any and every circumstance I have learned the secret of being filled and going hungry, both of having abundance and suffering need.

Philippians 4:12 NASV

Surviving prosperity with our values intact is indeed a learned skill that must be carefully developed. Joseph's story (like many of ours) contains elements of abasement and abundance, of humble means and prosperity. After great suffering and injustice he was eventually elevated to a position of prominence, because he had been faithful in the little things, the things no one was aware of but God. Then God gave Joseph the opportunity to be faithful in much bigger ways.

What did Joseph receive? First, he was given *prominence*. Pharaoh set him "over all the land of Egypt." His word was law extending farther than the eye could see. All of Egypt was under his authority. Joseph was a man to be reckoned with anywhere and everywhere. He had the power to effect change and make decisions that would determine the course of an entire nation. He was important. He was somebody. Today we would say he had clout.

Second, he was given financial *power*. You've probably heard this twist on the golden rule: "He who has the gold, rules." Joseph "had the gold" in the form of the signet ring that Pharaoh had taken from his own hand and placed on the hand of his new prime minister. With the ring, Joseph had the authority to stamp PAID across the face of every bill that crossed Pharaoh's desk. The etymology of the word *signet* means "to sink down," and the signet ring would sink down into the sealing wax on a document, making the sign of the royal head of state. Possessing the ring meant having signatory authority in all financial matters.

Finally, Pharaoh gave Joseph the *prestige* befitting his position by dressing him in fine linen and a golden necklace and allowing him to ride in his second chariot in all official Egyptian "motorcades." (He might even have had a personalized license plate that simply read "2"!) With his social status came political control as well. Wherever he went criers would precede him shouting, "Bow the knee!" (The modern-day equivalent of this might be the frustrating, "Hold for Mr. Big, please.") The trappings of wealth and power belonged to Joseph just as they did to Pharaoh.

While it might seem that Joseph was set for life following these events, the real truth is that he was in more danger in the palace than he ever faced in the pit or in prison. Maintaining perspective when God exalts us is incredibly difficult. Many in the evangelical church today have no trouble praying for someone who is down and out. The suffering, the hungry, the homeless, the disenfranchised, and the abused are quick to make our prayer lists and rightfully so. (We are quick to pray for *ourselves* in any of these circumstances too.) But something seems to happen to our levels of commitment and concern when either we or they attain a certain level of prosperity.

Material wealth and success may be the deadliest dangers of our time. In the workplace, ego, power, position, and profit are gods that are worshipped with frightening resolve and consistency. Money is not the root of all evil, but loving it is. It is the *desire* for power, not power itself, that destroys individuals, marriages, and families. Joseph did not seek to become prime minister of Egypt at any cost. God placed Joseph in that position, and Joseph remained faithful to Him there.

Many Christians who obtain success are tempted to drift away from the Bible-preaching church (or bail out of it altogether!), because of those legalistic folks who believe you cannot love Jesus and drive a new car. Joseph proved that it is possible to love God and have wealth, power, and prestige.

There is a false gospel of success and prosperity being proclaimed today, and I am not an advocate of it. But I do believe that God has gifted some to be materially successful men and women, and that one who is so gifted must use that gift for the glory of God and not for personal gain or self-aggrandizement.

*M*aterial wealth and success may be the deadliest dangers of our time.

The Gospel of Mark records the story of a couple of status-seeking disciples who learned a lesson in humility from the most powerful person they had ever known. When the mother of James and John, the two sons of Zebedee, approached Jesus with a request that her boys be granted places of prestige at His right and left hands, His anger must have been a complete shock to all within earshot:

> "You do not know what you ask. Are you able to
> drink the cup that I drink, and be baptized with

the baptism that I am baptized with?" They said to Him, "We are able." So Jesus said to them, "You will indeed drink the cup that I drink, and with the baptism I am baptized with you will be baptized; but to sit on My right hand and on My left is not Mine to give, but it is for those for whom it is prepared.... You know that those who are considered rulers over the Gentiles lord it over them, and their great ones exercise authority over them. Yet it shall not be so among you; but whoever desires to become great among you shall be your servant. And whoever of you desires to be first shall be slave of all. For even the Son of Man did not come to be served, but to serve, and to give His life a ransom for many.

Mark 10:38–45

While power in a worldly sense is a thing to desire and wield, in God's economy power's purpose is strictly for service.

James and John wanted the prestige and recognition of being exalted with Jesus as His chosen ones. But Jesus warned that the price of power is great, and its implicit responsibility is greater still. His anger to these two ambitious followers reveals that while power in a worldly sense is a thing to desire and wield, in God's economy power's purpose is strictly for service. It is not a thing to be desired and held but to be used up and given away. Regardless of the way in which it is used, power presents a personal challenge to every believer, and to meet its challenge we must understand it.

Power is attractive

Researchers at Syracuse University in New York reported recently that a man's earning power and success are more attractive to women than a handsome profile! In other words in their survey an average looking guy in a designer suit and a Rolex watch was rated as more attractive than a Mel Gibson look-alike in a janitor's uniform. According to Dr. John M. Townsend, "Women are more attracted to signs of success and prowess" in a potential mate. "In the prehistoric hunting-gathering band, it was the successful hunter they were turned on to."

When asked to explain the public's apparent fascination with him, flamboyant power-broker Donald Trump said, "It's a look, it's an age, it's a style, it's a success. I'm the youngest. People that are wealthier than me are in their seventies." Trump, a native of Queens, a self-made celebrity fond of referring to himself in the third person, seems obsessed with acquiring things— airlines, casinos, and high-rise buildings—and putting his name on them. His voracious appetite for power prompted a self-proclaimed friend to observe, "He's so exclusively involved with himself, with his need to announce and re-announce himself, that there's no room for another person."

*N*o amount of success makes a man sovereign. Only God is sovereign.

In using power and financial success to feed his ego, Trump inadvertently orchestrated his own downfall. Now his business crises and well-publicized divorce (and not his billion dollar deals) are making the headlines. "The Donald," who was once the darling of investors and financiers, vividly proves the truth of these words from the book of James: "For where jealousy and selfish ambition exist, there is disorder and every evil thing."

Power is tempting

The tempting appeal of power lies in the belief that it can change or eliminate difficult circumstances. No amount of power or success makes a man sovereign. Only God is sovereign. Satan, knowing well the lure of power, tried to entice Jesus with it while He was alone in the wilderness preparing for His earthly assignment. The temptation presented to Christ was not to gain power, but to use the power He already had as the Son of God to care for Himself, win the acceptance of men, and gain personal glory. He refused on all three counts. For those who have been blessed with great personal power or success, the temptations will be similar.

When the tempter came to Jesus saying, "If You are the Son of God, command that these stones become bread," he was simply suggesting that Christ use His power to meet His own personal needs, rather than depend on God to sustain Him. It is so easy when we have plenty to believe that our success makes us self-sufficient, but that is a lie.

Satan's second proposition to Christ was that he throw Himself down from the pinnacle of the temple, since "He [God] will give His angels charge concerning You, and on their hands they will bear You up, lest You strike Your foot against a stone." Jesus' response was that it would be wrong for Him to stage a sensational rescue as a test for God. While such a phenomenon might have netted Him followers, it would have been based on the incorrect premise that we can manipulate God for our own ends. Our power-hungry, Machiavellian world says that the end justifies the means. The gospel says that it does not.

Finally Jesus' tempter suggested that if Jesus would worship him, Jesus Himself would be exalted and glorified. Satan tried to convince Jesus of the subtle lie that there are many acceptable objects for our worship. Satan never explicitly said, "Stop worshipping God and worship me exclusively," but Jesus knew that God and God alone deserved His worship. "Begone, Satan! For it is written, 'You shall worship the Lord your God and serve Him only.'"

The truth is that we cannot seek out power and prosperity and worship God at the same time. Why? Because "no one can serve two masters; for either he will hate the one and love the other, or else he will be loyal to the one and despise the other. You cannot serve God and mammon" (Matt. 6:24). In the kingdom divided loyalty is not loyalty to God at all; it is loyalty to the opposition and betrayal of all He stands for.

Instead of using His power at the beginning of His earthly ministry to achieve prominence, Jesus proved His power as He appropriated every ounce of it in Gethsemane to submit to the will of His Father. Only through such power could He become the suffering servant who would die for the sins of a lost world.

*P*ower and success are not trophies— they're tools.

Power is lethal when misused

Power and success are not trophies—they're tools. Like any tool they must be used correctly to achieve the desired results, and they can become dangerous when they are misused. A band saw can help a carpenter construct fine furniture, but in the hands of a child the same piece of equipment becomes a dangerous weapon. He will not be able to use it correctly. Codeine and morphine are valuable medications when properly prescribed by physicians to alleviate severe pain, but they are not recommended for constant or careless use. Why? Because they become potentially addictive and deadly when taken in excess.

Before he became their national nightmare, the German people perceived Adolf Hitler as their savior. The power he might have used to unify and strengthen Germany, he instead distorted to meet his own insatiable need for control and to effect the murder of millions whom he considered unfit or inferior. Power misused is a fearful thing.

Joseph stands out in history as a man who successfully handled prosperity. He did not abuse or flaunt the power bestowed on him as a thirty-year-old foreigner in a pagan land. Instead he used it to serve those he could have exploited. How could this young man have been so adequately prepared for his tremendous role? A. W. Tozer once said that God cannot greatly use anyone who He has not allowed to be deeply hurt. Joseph had been hurt, abused, shamed, and embarrassed as he grew and made his way from the pit to the palace, to prison and back again to prominence. As Potiphar's servant, Joseph was placed in control of all the household. As a prisoner, he was placed in control of all the jail. Finally Joseph was placed in control of all of Egypt. And in every circumstance, he prospered.

God uses whatever it takes to get our attention and to get us in tune with Him. With His hammer He will pound us and mold us into the shape He alone can see. With His file He patiently grinds away at our rough edges. Then He puts us into the fire of the furnace. The process is often painful, but it is absolutely essential if we are to fulfill His plan for us. Adversity prepares us to be victorious in prosperity, and Joseph knew what it was to be tempered by the living God.

Sculptor Gutzon Borglum, creator of the famous faces we see today on Mount Rushmore, was once asked how he created an image in stone. He replied that the process was simply one of removing what did not belong from a sheer face of rock. When Borglum hammered and chiseled away at a slab of granite, removing large and small pieces of it, eventually only the image he first envisioned remained. What might seem destructive during the creation process can be seen later to be an integral part of the artist's grand design. So it is with us and with the Sculptor of our lives.

Mississippi Boy Makes Good

God uses whatever it takes to get our attention and to get us in tune with Him.

Success has smiled on Johnny Baker, but it hasn't changed him, not one bit. Johnny grew up in Meridian, Mississippi, and attended Mississippi State on a football scholarship. He was a hard-working athlete, who went on to play professional ball for the Houston Oilers and the San Diego Chargers. Johnny married Carla, and today the Bakers have four children, Jason, Cara, Jacob, and Joshua.

Following his retirement from professional football, Johnny began to work in investments and real estate, and for an old country boy he has done very well. God has blessed the Bakers richly with material success, but for as long as I have known Johnny, no matter what he had, he has been a giver. He would be embarrassed if I told you the details of his generosity to our church and to the host of nameless individuals he has helped through the years.

The world counts Johnny a big success. His business has prospered, and he has enjoyed the accolades of a professional sports career as well. Every now and then you'll see his name in the local paper, but if you want to know about Johnny, you'll learn more about him from his friends than his press clippings. You might ask the shoe shine man at a country club in our city where the well-heeled set golfs. He knows Johnny as the man who calls him "sir" out of respect for his age, and says that while most folks just toss their shoes at him and expect a job well done, Johnny talks to him like he's somebody, because to Johnny he is!

Or you could ask one of the hundred or so members of the adult Sunday school class Johnny co-teaches what stands out about him, and they would tell you it's not his money or his worldly success but his love for the Word of God. If you asked his family, they would tell you that Johnny makes time for them, that no deal is more important than his wife or his children and their interests and needs.

God has blessed Johnny Baker with the kind of material resources few of us will ever see, but he treats the "nobody" and the "somebody" with equal respect, and he's not ruled by his possessions in the least. You'd be right at home jogging or hunting with this old Mississippi boy, because people love Johnny and he loves them right back!

How to Handle Prosperity

When prosperity comes, the way we respond to it is critical. The following four principles often determine whether or not we will survive power and success as men and women of God. They are warnings to heed when we're on top of the world.

Beware of believing your own press clippings

T. S. Eliot once said that half the harm done in the world is done by people who want to feel important. Success is heady stuff because it feeds the part of our ego that needs to be stroked, to feel important. One danger of having gained some measure of power or success is that once it comes, we may begin to overestimate our own significance or to believe our own press clippings.

When New York City tabloids quoted Donald Trump's girlfriend regarding his reputation as a modern-day Don Juan, Trump contended that one could be accused of worse. "The *Post* headline today, well, you could take it as a great compliment," he said. Some insist that the sensational reports were taken in just that way. "I guarantee that headline is one of the highlights of his adult life," said one associate. "He loves it. He'd put it up on his wall, next to all the magazine covers, if he thought he could get away with it."

When Joseph became Egypt's number two man, he avoided the delusion that he was something exceptional. We know, because during this time he was given an Egyptian wife and became a father, and the names he gave his sons provide wonderful insight into the steadfastness of his character. He named his first son Manasseh, meaning "to forget," "for God has made me forget all my toil and all my father's house" (Gen. 41:51). God was the one who had made Joseph forget the sting of a past that was difficult, and He received all the credit for Joseph's present satisfaction. Although he remembered the former injustices and the hard times, Joseph forgot their sting. That is something a self-centered person can never do.

God was the one who had made Joseph forget the sting of a past that was difficult, and He received all the credit for Joseph's present satisfaction.

In choosing the name Ephraim for his second son, Joseph was literally saying that God had blessed him. He said, "For God has caused me to be fruitful in the land of my affliction" (Gen. 41:52). Again Joseph points to God as the one who caused the difficulties of his life to result in untold blessing. Nothing about either name suggests that Joseph is full of himself, blinded by the prestige of his new position. Instead he proves himself humble and grateful to God, who has provided for him.

Beware of falling prey to your own appetites

Douglas LaBier is a Washington, D.C., psychotherapist with an unusual practice. Many of his patients are what he calls "troubled winners," men and women who have lasted on the fast track of their careers, but who are paying the price emotionally. LaBier's working wounded clientele have found that hard-won career success and achievement lead to emptiness and despair as often as they do to happiness and fulfillment. "A life too much devoted to pursuing money, power, position, and control over others," says LaBier, "ends up being emotionally impoverished."

When all of a man or a woman's energy is spent in reaching the top, it is a crushing blow to realize that "the top" is seldom what it's cracked up to be. An appetite to be the best is fed by many corporations and institutions and applauded by a watching world, but it is an appetite that is never completely satiated, no matter how well it is fed. In fact, our present generation may be the first in history to reach the limits of satisfaction that materialism can provide. New psychological catch phrases, like "success depression," "affluenza," and "the Big Chill Syndrome," speak volumes about the emptiness of blind ambition.

There's an old adage that for every one person who can handle success there are ten who can handle failure. The biblical account of God's anointed David is just one example of the difficulties of success. Before he became king, David lived on the run from Saul, who sought to kill him at every turn. Even with a price on his head David remained a man of God. His repeated refusal to seize the crown from Saul indicated that his heart belonged steadfastly to the Lord.

Then this man after God's own heart became king, and disaster struck. Instead of going out to battle with his army, David stayed at the palace and succumbed to the role of "peeping Tom" as he watched his next-door neighbor take a bath. Casually, almost imperceptably, the sin of adultery entered David's life. When he was at the very height of his power, David fell prey to his own appetite for sin.

A person with power has two choices. The power can be used to promote self, or it can be used to serve others.

Beware of abusing power for personal gain

A person with power has two choices. The power can be used to promote self, or it can be used to serve others. The world chooses the first option every time. The second choice is the way of the Cross. The goal and priority of the Christian should be to live for God before everything else, and that includes climbing the corporate ladder.

Because we live in an "every man for himself" world, the idea of denying self for the good of another is completely foreign to most of us. Charles Colson, in his book *Loving God*, asserts that even among friends or co-conspirators, loyalty to self is stronger than loyalty to others. The "natural human instinct for self-preservation was so overwhelming," he says, "that the [Watergate] conspirators . . . a small band of hand-picked loyalists, could not hold a conspiracy together for more than two weeks."

Without accountability it is far too easy for one in power to use that privilege to elevate or protect himself, and often at the expense of others. The ultimate authority, of course, is the authority of God, and the person who lives in submission to Him, as Joseph did, will put a protective hedge between himself and the temptation to abuse power.

For the Christian Jesus sets the ultimate example of right use of power, as the apostle Paul relates in Philippians 2:5–8, "Let this mind be in you which was also in Christ Jesus, who, being in the form of God, did not consider it robbery to be equal with God, but made Himself of no reputation, taking the form of a bondservant, and coming in the likeness of men. And being found in appearance as a man, He humbled Himself and became obedient to the point of death, even the death of the cross."

Jesus' job description was simple: obey the Father. Anything that might hinder His ability to obey was eliminated from His life, including self-interest. The paradox exhibited in the lives of those who follow Him is that by denying self, by laying aside power, we can become victorious and for the first time genuinely discover our true selves as God intended us to be. Neither adversity nor success will defeat us when our priorities are biblically based.

Joseph learned the same premise that Paul later stated as the basis of his life: He learned to be content in every circumstance, and he also discovered that the one constant in life is the love of God. That nothing— neither "death nor life, nor angels nor principalities nor powers, nor things present nor things to come, nor height nor depth, nor any other created thing," can separate us from that love. Not even power, because, as has been rightly said, "The only cure for the love of power is the power of love."

Prosperity

- Prosperity tests us in a way that adversity seldom can, displaying character flaws that never surface when we're under fire.
- Our level of commitment to God can shrink in proportion to our drive to get ahead if we are not attentive to that possibility.
- Real status is achieved through servanthood. Even Jesus took the servant's role instead of aspiring to positions of prestige within the religious community of His time.
- Money and power are not antidotes to trouble, and no amount of success makes a man sovereign. Only God is sovereign.
- The misuse of power can be lethal. Success is a tool to enable us to do good, not a trophy to be admired by those less fortunate.

Chapter 10

Emotional Acid

Dealing with Guilt

Then Joseph said to them the third day, "Do this and live, for I fear God: If you are honest men, let one of your brothers be confined to your prison house; but you, go and carry grain for the famine of your houses. And bring your youngest brother to me; so your words will be verified, and you shall not die." And they did so. Then they said to one another, "We are truly guilty concerning our brother, for we saw the anguish of his soul when he pleaded with us, and we would not hear; therefore this distress has come upon us."

Genesis 42:18–21

Emotional Acid

Guilt is one of the most powerful emotions we experience. Its influence is frightenly pervasive, and its staying power is tremendous. It can literally live unexamined and seemingly unfed for years. Christian psychiatrist Dr. Frank Minirth likens guilt to an "emotional acid" that can act as a constructive or destructive force in our lives. While you and I may manipulate feelings of guilt in order to shame ourselves or others, almost always with negative results, God uses guilt like an engraver uses acid—in small doses to clean, refine, and perfect His original design.

*G*od uses guilt like an engraver uses acid— in small doses to clean, refine, and perfect His original design.

When the worldwide famine in Pharoah's dream came to pass, the Egyptian storehouses were full, thanks to Joseph's administration. His half-brothers even found themselves traveling to Egypt to buy grain. Nearly twenty-five years had passed since his brothers had sold Joseph into slavery. Jacob was now an old and ailing man who had to be carried by his sons from place to place. The years of sorrow and grief over the loss of his favorite son had taken their toll on him. How many times did he take that old bloodstained coat out and turn it over in his hands, tormented by the memory of the day it was returned with the tragic news that his son was dead?

*S*in has a way of aging us.

The brothers themselves were now middle-aged men—tan, weathered shepherds with full beards and calloused hands. They must have looked older than their years, too, because sin has a way of aging us. For years they had carried a terrible secret that was seldom discussed and never revealed, even among themselves. Little did they know, no one bought grain in Egypt without speaking with Joseph and they were about to come face-to-face with their secret and their guilt.

But Joseph was a different story. Joseph, sold years before and given up as dead, was now the prime minister of Egypt. He lived a life of incredible wealth and prosperity. A walk about his home with this former slave would reveal just how far he had come. He lived in a palace with walls paneled in beautiful acacia wood. It was furnished with skillfully carved ebony furniture and intricately woven rugs and the skins of exotic animals covered cool marble floors. Outside spacious courtyards were dotted with sycamore and palm trees and accented by flowing fountains. Choirs sang melodic hymns, accompanied by musicians on lutes, harps, and violins.

The years had been kind to Joseph, but he had not forgotten his past. He longed to see his father again and to know what had become of his younger brother, Benjamin, and his older half-brothers. Had Jacob been as unwise in showing his preference for Benjamin as he had with Joseph? Without his mother, Rachel, who died when he was born, had Benjamin suffered harm from the others?

At this emotionally loaded juncture, God used the well-aged guilt carried by Joseph's brothers to bring His ultimate plan to fruition. Remember God's promise to Abraham years before? "I will make of your seed a chosen nation." To do that God needed these ten sin-hardened men! He employed the emotional acid of guilt to pierce their cold, indifferent hearts, and moved them to take their entire family to Egypt where He could begin to shape them into His covenant people.

Left to their own devices, Egypt was the last place these men would have chosen to go. Just the mention of the word must have sent chills up and down their spines! They knew that the Ishmaelites, who had taken Joseph away, meant to sell him there as a slave. But they were hungry, and their children were hungry, and there was grain in Egypt.

The story of their journey to Egypt and their fateful meeting with Joseph centers around one immutable truth: Buried guilt lives. Years before Jacob's older sons had buried Joseph alive in a pit and had tried to bury their guilt along with him. But the truth is, we do not bury sin. We carry it with us. If we do not allow God to deal with our past sins, we carry the weight of them wherever we go. And no one else has to know, because *we* know.

*I*f we do not allow God to deal with our past sins, we carry the weight of them wherever we go.

The title character in Shakespeare's drama *Macbeth* is a vivid example of this truth. Macbeth wanted to be king of Scotland so desperately that he was willing to commit murder to gain the throne. He and Lady Macbeth hatched a plan and carried it out with apparent success. And all would have been well, except the murderer seemed to waver on the brink of insanity, and his accomplice could not stop washing her hands! No one knew their secret, but she saw herself as stained by the blood they had spilled and he was crazy with guilt.

> Now does he feel
> His secret murders sticking on his hands.
> Now minutely revolts upbraid his faith-breach.
> Those he commands move only in command,
> Nothing in love. Now does he feel his title
> Hang loose about him, like a giant's robe
> Upon a dwarfish thief.[1]

We can attempt to alleviate our guilt with rationalization, activity, and the passage of time, but nothing changes the fact that sin undealt with by God lives forever. We can rename it, bury it, ignore it, or explain it away, but the bottom line is that sin—and the guilt that accompanies it—never dies until God gets hold

*S*in—and the guilt that accompanies it—never dies until God gets hold of it.

of it. Until He does, we can expect to see our same tired sin all over again in a different time and place, like the recurring sequel to a movie we never liked to begin with!

I have seen more damage done to individuals and relationships by the ghost of guilt than from any other source. Frequently the guilt of some past sin is carried from generation to generation, affecting the lives of those who may be totally unaware of its origin. In London's Gatwick Airport (and in many foreign airports) baggage or parcels that are found unattended and unclaimed are seized by authorities, because terrorists have been known to hide explosives in luggage and then abandon it. Unclaimed luggage does not just sit forever, and psychologists tell us that guilt and shame do not go unclaimed either. If a parent refuses his or her own guilt, a child will often subconsciously pick it up and carry it.

What Guilt Does

What does guilt look like? How does it affect us? I think guilt can best be identified by four specific things that it does.

Guilt paralyzes us

The Bible tells us that when the sons of Jacob learned there was grain in Egypt, they did nothing. This prompted Jacob to ask them why they were standing around staring at each other! Ignorant of their long-standing deceit, he could not understand their reticence, and he certainly didn't understand how an innocent trip to Egypt to buy food would involve such difficult decision making. They would have preferred another solution to their hunger—any solution but a trip to Egypt, because going there meant they would recall the sin they had committed against their brother, Joseph, years before.

I know parents who have made mistakes in their pasts that they seem powerless to warn their children against. The guilt of their actions is so heavy, they are unable to do anything when their offspring experience difficulty in the same areas. David is an excellent biblical example of this crippling aspect of guilt. He was strangely silent when his son Amnon raped his daughter Tamar (you will remember that David's track record with sexual indiscretion was less than exemplary). And when son Absalom sought justice by killing Amnon, again David was silent. (Perhaps he remembered plotting the murder of Uriah, the Hittite?)

How sad that our old guilt paralyzes us and keeps us from moving ahead in life. It was hunger that finally brought Joseph's brothers back to the scene of their crime. When we're hungry enough, we'll go anywhere, but it takes an enormous appetite to break the inertia of a guilt-ridden man.

Guilt distorts our vision

Joseph's brothers did not recognize him when they came before him to buy grain, but he knew them immediately.

He chose not to reveal himself to them right away. He had so many questions about them: Had their hearts changed toward him? Did they regret what they had done? What about Jacob and Benjamin? Were they alive and well? Joseph decided it was best that his identity remain secret for a while. Actually he accused them first of being spies—a charge they vehemently denied, claiming that they were honest men. "Your servants are twelve brothers, the sons of one man in the land of Canaan; and in fact, the youngest is with our father today, and one is no more."

*B*uried guilt keeps us from seeing things as they really are.

Buried guilt keeps us from seeing things as they really are. In our self-absorption, we have a hard time maintaining the proper focus on the world around us.

When author and theologian Frederick Buechner wrote a brief, fictionalized account of his father's suicide, some twenty years after the fact in *The Return of Ansel Gibbs*, his mother reacted with unexpected fury. According to Buechner it was as if he had betrayed a sacred trust. "I felt as much a traitor as she charged me with being," he said, "and at the age of thirty-two was as horrified at what I had done as if I had been a child of ten. I was full of guilt and remorse and sure that in who-knows-what grim and lasting way I would be made to suffer for what I had done."

All Buechner had done was simply tell the truth, but old guilt and shame over the circumstances of his father's death caused him and his mother to see that as a grave (and unforgivable) sin. Buried guilt can so mar our perspective that we eventually become unable to discern truth from error, the real from the imagined.

Guilt blinds us from the truth

Face to face with Joseph once more, his brothers spoke these words of introduction: "Your servants are twelve brothers, the sons of one man in the land of Canaan; and in fact, the youngest is with our father today, and one is no more." *One is no more.* It was an interesting confession. It told Joseph that Benjamin and Jacob were alive. And it told him what the brothers thought must have become of him: "One is no more."

These men had told the twenty-five year-old story of Joseph's being killed by a wild animal so many times in the intervening years, they had come to believe it themselves. By this time, they would not have recognized the truth if it had knocked them down!

Although they might not have realized it, these brothers were about as honest as the fellow who reluctantly found himself a celebrity for returning a large sum of "found" money. It seems that a man and his girlfriend went into a fast-food restaurant and ordered a sack of chicken to go. Moments earlier the manager had placed all the day's cash receipts in a bag and set it at the side of the serving counter. When the clerk reached for the couple's order, by mistake he picked up the bag of money. They paid for the chicken, got in their car, and drove to a park for a picnic. When they opened the bag there were no drumsticks, but there were lots of past presidents!

After talking briefly about their find, the couple decided that the right thing to do was to return the money. When they arrived at the restaurant, they were greeted by a very happy manager. "I can't believe it," he said. "I'm calling the papers. They'll take your picture and run the story for sure. You've got to be the two most honest people in the entire state!" The young man replied, "No, please don't call the paper! You see I'm a married man, and this woman is not my wife."

Guilt can make our truth-telling selective, causing us to ignore facts we would like to forget and to change our message depending on the audience we face.

> *Guilt can make our truth-telling selective, causing us to ignore facts we would like to forget and to change our message depending on the audience we face.*

Guilt imprisons us in the past

Although Joseph (and not his brothers) had spent time in prison, the brothers were captive in a way that Joseph never was. While he was behind bars, Joseph was nevertheless free from the shackles of guilt that bound the rest of Jacob's bunch. His pain at being locked up for a crime he didn't commit (the assault of Potiphar's wife) was nothing compared to their agony of remembering.

Joseph saw their guilt for himself when he demanded to see Benjamin. He held the cards because he had what they wanted—food. As "payment" Joseph requested to see Benjamin. When he did, they began whispering to one another. He understood every word they said, although they didn't know it. He was amazed that their first response to his demand was an overwhelming sense of guilt. After all these years and all the lies, the guilt had not disappeared. "This has happened to us because of what we did to Joseph," one reasoned. And then Reuben played "I told you so" and insisted that their current dilemma was an accounting for Joseph's blood.

His heart felt so heavy as he saw their guilt and fear, he had to turn away. Tears stung his eyes and washed his cheeks. His life had been difficult in the years since he left Canaan, but no circumstance he faced could match the pain his brothers must have endured as a result of their sin against Joseph. Guilt was one pain he never experienced, and he was incredibly thankful for that in their presence.

When he turned back to them, he took Simeon and bound him before their eyes. Then Joseph ordered his servants to fill their bags with grain and to restore each one's money to his sack. He gave them provisions for their journey and sent them on their way. After they had gone a short distance, one of the brothers opened his sack and was shocked to find his money—all of it—inside. When he told the others, each examined his own sack. When they saw that all of their money had been returned, they were filled with fear, saying, "What is this that God has done to us?"

In Joseph's meeting with his brothers, he invoked the name of God: "Then Joseph said to them the third day, 'Do this and live, for I fear God.'" There is nothing he could have said that would have frightened these guilty men more than to mention God. The sound of it must have been like the touch of a hot iron on their collective conscience!

Too many of us today live chained to the past by guilty memories, like the 2,000 pound circus elephant anchored in place by a bicycle chain on a stake. When he was young he couldn't pull the stake out of the ground, no matter how he tugged and pulled. So after a while he quit trying. Now you and I both know that a big elephant should have no trouble getting free from a small chain on a stake, but memory keeps him there.

Satan loves to remind you and me of our former struggles and failures. He is always ready to whisper them to us or bring out old "home movies" of our sins. What he never tells us is that we are no longer guilty of any sin we have confessed and repented, no matter how heinous it was. It simply has no more power, and God does not remember it.

Living with the Ghost of Guilt

A young member of our church staff, I'll call her Renee, knows better than many how powerful the ghost of guilt can be until it is dealt with honestly before God. Renee accepted Christ as her Savior at age ten, but she admits that the "lordship" part of that commitment did not materialize until well into adulthood. Life threw this young woman some rough curves while she was still a teenager, including the sudden, unexpected death of her mother.

The summer before her sophomore year of college, Renee discovered she was pregnant. Her high school sweetheart was not prepared for this news, and he left her to deal with it alone. She chose not to tell her father, dreading his disappointment in her and convinced he could not handle another heartbreak so soon after the death of his wife. Instead, she made an appointment at a local clinic and had an abortion. That done, she jumped headfirst into her sophomore year.

She was active in her sorority and began dating another young man, determined to enjoy all that college had to offer. She began to grow closer to her father as together they dealt with the trials involved in raising her two younger brothers without a mother in the home. Renee attended church on a semi-regular basis, although she says she did so more to make herself feel better than to foster real growth in her Christian life.

Thoughts of the abortion were never far away, in spite of the whirlwind of activity Renee surrounded herself with. She longed to share what she had been through with her father, but fourteen months after the death of her mother, at the age of forty-two, he suffered a massive heart attack. When it was determined that stress played a significant part in his condition Renee left college and returned home to care for him and her two younger brothers. Once again she decided her father was in no condition to hear about her abortion.

Renee recalls that many of her actions at that time were the direct result of the deep-rooted guilt she could not escape over the child she had aborted. In an attempt to prove that she could and would be a good wife and mother she became engaged to marry a man she never believed loved her. She "mothered" her dad and brothers, attempting to make herself feel better by giving them the care they so needed at the time. But when her engagement was broken and her father remarried all avenues of nurturing were taken away, and it was then that she began to feel the hurt of the guilt she carried in a way she could not avoid.

Although Renee had resumed her college career and outwardly appeared fine, inwardly she was depressed and fearful. She recalls calling her father one day and asking if he had ever had a nervous breakdown, because she thought that was what was happening to her. Her entire body seemed to shut down, and she ceased to function as a responsible person. After withdrawing from school with only finals to complete, she packed her bags and returned home to her father, her brothers, a new step-mother, and two step-sisters, whom she had met only twice before.

The next six weeks were spent sleeping twelve to fourteen hours a day and watching television for hours on end. Renee says she was so emotionally dead that it was an effort to perform the most basic functions. Attempts to discuss anything with her father regarding the reasons for her withdrawal from school and her depression led to bouts of uncontrolled weeping. She thought that if she rested more, she would get "back to normal." At the end of six weeks Renee's father announced that she should be able to return to school, take a full course load, and make up the incompletes she received in her last semester. Although the thought of returning to school made her physically ill and she begged to be allowed to stay at home, he insisted that she either go back to college or find a job. Reluctantly, she returned to school.

Back at school Renee received permission from the dean to take only nine hours while she completed her work from the previous semester, but she was by no means out of the woods. She recalls that simply getting out of bed was a huge struggle. She attended class, ate, slept, and exercised, but did little else. Her weight fluctuated dramatically as she gained and lost twenty pounds in a four-month period. She went home as frequently as she could, leaving school on Thursday evening each week and not returning until just before her Tuesday morning class.

Longing to "come clean" to someone, Renee finally told an aunt about the abortion. But she "changed the details to protect the innocent," saying that she had been raped and became pregnant as a result. Any relief she felt from this confession was short-lived, however, as the aunt and her husband went to the police to determine whether or not Renee had reported a rape. They learned, of course, that she had not. They gently confronted her with their findings, and the flood gates finally broke as Renee poured out her heart to them and allowed them to lead her in a prayer asking for God's forgiveness.

The blessing of being relieved of an old sin was wonderful, but Renee says it was just the beginning of her healing process. A pastor who counseled her during this time explained that getting right with God was the first step, but that she needed to go to her father and her ex-boyfriend and seek their forgiveness as well. For the next six months Renee practiced telling her father, and primed him through cards and letters for the story she would soon share with him. Finally her father (who had moved out of state) was back in Texas on a house-hunting trip and insisted that he and Renee have dinner to clear the air.

Renee says that as soon as they were seated at the table, he asked her to explain all the cryptic messages of the last six months. She took a deep breath and plunged in. "What would you say if I told you I had gotten pregnant and had an abortion?" The next few moments of silence were heavy, but Renee says that as she looked at her father, she saw only love in his face.

With tears in his eyes, he responded with these words: "I only wish I'd been there for you during such a difficult time." No words of disappointment. No condemnation. Only a desire to let her know she was loved and forgiven. Renee's sense of relief was overwhelming.

In spite of her confession, the difficulties were not over. The consequences of living a lie for two years were not erased just because she had come clean. It was not until nearly five years after the abortion that she finally worked through all the phases of her guilt and grief. She became involved in church for the right reasons, and began to learn what it means to have a personal relationship with Jesus Christ. She began to spend several hours each week counseling at a crisis pregnancy center, sharing her story time and time again with young girls who were in situations similar to the one she had faced.

*N*o matter how marred our performance may be, if we confess our mistakes, we are eligible for God's forgiveness.

Today Renee would tell you that God is good and that He uses even our mistakes to His glory. The road back from guilt is a long one, but it is possible to exchange condemnation for comfort and forgiveness, and to be out from under the crushing weight of buried guilt once and for all!

Steps for Dealing with Buried Sin

If you are struggling today with the ghost of guilt, these steps for dealing with this powerful emotion can help you.

Admit your guilt

No matter how marred our performance may be, if we confess our mistakes, we are eligible for God's forgiveness. First John 1:9 says, "If we confess our sins, He is faithful and just to forgive us our sins and to cleanse us from all unrighteousness." Forgiveness and healing are not possible without confession. It is the key to wholeness, and we hold it in our own hands.

*A*fter we own our sin by admitting it and asking God for forgiveness, we need to accept the forgiveness He offers based on Christ's sacrificial death on our behalf.

It is no coincidence that meetings for those struggling with alcoholism begin with the spoken admission "I am an alcoholic." The confession itself is a beginning point in the recovery process. Dr. Paul Tournier says, in his psychological study *Guilt and Grace,* that "the painful path of humiliation and guilt, with all the heartache and rebellion against God which it brings, is the very path which opens on to the royal road of grace." The more aware we are of guilt, the more we will know of grace.

How do we go about the business of confession? We begin by getting alone with God and letting His Spirit reveal to us the condition of our hearts. David invited this kind of divine inspection when he prayed in Psalm 139, "Search me, O God, and know my heart; / Try me, and know my anxieties; / And see if there is any wicked way in me." If we are open to Him, the Holy Spirit will convict us of sin and make us aware of things we may have subconsciously covered up in the process.

Once these things are revealed, we admit they are our responsibility and confess them to the One they are offensive to. In the days of the Old Testament when the sacrificial system was in place for Israel, a Jew would bring animals to the temple to be sacrificed to ensure unbroken fellowship with God. The sacrificial laws were specific, so many would know by the animal or animals brought and the way they were sacrificed what a worshipper's particular sin was. When the animal was brought to the altar, the

Jew laid his hands on it in identification, as if to say, "This is mine." In the same way we are to identify with our own sin and confess that it is ours and no one else's, understanding that the One we sin against is God.

Accept forgiveness

After we own our sin by admitting it and asking God for forgiveness, we need to accept the forgiveness He offers based on Christ's sacrificial death on our behalf. Accepting forgiveness is perhaps the most difficult aspect of guilt. It is so hard for those of us who were brought up in a merit-oriented society to truly believe that we do not have to earn forgiveness. The fact is we cannot earn it, we can only receive it. There is nothing we can add to the payment Jesus Christ made for our sins, either past, present, or future.

How do we know when we have truly accepted forgiveness? When we acknowledge our sin and are offered and accept forgiveness, relationship is restored. There is no hiding, no avoidance, no rationalizing, or excusing. This is one of the secrets of the life of David, a man whose days were marked by a deep, abiding love relationship with God. David made many of the same mistakes we make today (hopefully ours will not be recorded for future generations of readers!), but he was faithful to admit his guilt and to ask God for forgiveness, because he wanted his relationship with God to be restored.

Most of us were taught as children how to graciously receive gifts. We learned to say thank you, write thank-you notes, and express appreciation for what we were given. I can't remember a single birthday or Christmas in my life that I have failed to take home the gifts I was given. At our house unwrapped gifts don't stay under the Christmas tree all year. They are given to be used, worn, enjoyed, and they are. Forgiveness is a gift from God, a costly one, but the price has already been paid. Our responsibility is to receive it with a thankful heart, knowing that we can add nothing to its value.

Forgive others

There is a standing order for any man or woman who has freely received the gift of forgiveness from God: Forgive one another. If I accept God's forgiveness and then refuse to forgive someone else, I am operating on the basis of a double standard. Jesus, in His Sermon on the Mount, instructed His disciples regarding forgiveness:

> For if you forgive men their trespasses, your heavenly Father will also forgive you. But if you do not forgive men their trespasses, neither will your Father forgive your trespasses.
>
> Matthew 6:14–15

Forgiveness can be understood as the release of a debt. By refusing to forgive, I keep others emotionally indebted to me. They feel like they have to pay up constantly for old grievances. This kind of living knows nothing about grace, and I cannot have an open, unhindered relationship with God if I am holding others hostage for something He would forgive me for.

I cannot have an open, unhindered relationship with God if I am holding others hostage for something He would forgive me for.

Joseph wisely understood this principle and refused to hold on to the hurt caused when his brothers sold him into slavery, saying, "But now, do not therefore be grieved or angry with yourselves because you sold me here; for God sent me before you to preserve life. . . . So now it was not you who sent me here, but God; and He has made me a father to Pharaoh, and lord of all his house, and a ruler throughout all the land of Egypt" (Gen. 45:5–8).

We cannot be unforgiving to others and right with God. He does not withhold our salvation from us, but fellowship with Him is broken when we refuse to extend forgiveness to those who have wronged us. It's easy to see how ridiculous this kind of thing is when we imagine someone who has hurt us asking both God and us for forgiveness at the same time. God readily says yes—who then are we to say no?

Walk in the light

Once we have worked through steps 1 through 3, we can know that God has forgiven our buried sin, and we can begin again to walk in the light of His love. No one, to my knowledge, has expressed this better than the apostle John in his first letter: "But if we walk in the light as He is in the light, we have fellowship with one another, and the blood of Jesus Christ His Son cleanses us from all sin" (1 John 1:7).

More than every once in a while, Houston gets a real gully-washer of a thunderstorm. The kind where thunder and lightning are heard and seen simultaneously, and the rain just comes down in sheets. Sometimes these storms, or "frog stranglers," result in power failure, which always seems to occur at the worst possible moment. In a church the size of ours, things can get dark in a hurry, even in broad daylight. Have you noticed how darkness shuts a lot of things down? Work ceases. Computer screens go dark. Conferences grind to a halt. Conversation even begins to wane. When the lights come back on activity begins again.

Our spiritual lives operate in much the same way. Away from the light of God's fellowship we are less alive. We need the warmth and illumination of His love to really live.

Has guilt separated you from someone you love? Has it separated you from God? Don't live another day with this "emotional acid" at work in your life. Choose instead to come clean and walk in the light of God's love. There is nothing—absolutely nothing—that He will not forgive through His Son Jesus Christ. Forgiveness and healing are ours for the asking.

Guilt

- People use guilt as a weapon to manipulate and intimidate; God uses conviction as a tool to perfect and strengthen His children.
- Unhandled guilt will not fade. It only intensifies and deepens with time. We can hide, deny, transfer, or ignore it, but only God can take it away.
- Guilt not dealt with can be a destructive legacy, handed down from one generation to another. It will not remain unclaimed.
- Guilt deceives, blinds us from the truth, distorts our perception, paralyzes us from taking action, and imprisons us in the past.
- With the blood of His only Son, God has paid for a way out of our individual prisons of guilt.

Chapter 11

Home Is Where the Heart Is

Forgiveness and Restoration

Then Joseph said to his brothers, "I am Joseph; does my father still live?" But his brothers could not answer him, for they were dismayed in his presence. And Joseph said to his brothers, "Please come near to me." So they came near. Then he said: "I am Joseph your brother, whom you sold into Egypt. . . .

So you shall tell my father of all my glory in Egypt, and of all that you have seen; and you shall hurry and bring my father down here." Then he fell on his brother Benjamin's neck and wept, and Benjamin wept on his neck. Moreover he kissed all his brothers and wept over them, and after that his brothers talked with him.

Genesis 45:3–4, 13–15

Home Is Where the Heart Is

Family reunions are a uniquely American tradition. Like baseball, apple pie, and the stars and stripes, they evoke a wave of nostalgia and foster a fierce affection for the place we know as home. The televised homecomings of the men and women of Operation Desert Storm captivated millions of us, and as proud Americans, we watched and cried day after day as returning soldiers were reunited with their joyful families.

Remember the scene? A military plane would touch down on a runway and cheering would begin. As the soldiers deplaned, their eyes searched the crowd for mothers, fathers, husbands, wives, children. Then amidst the long embraces, the tears, the hugs and kisses, a great many family reunions would begin simultaneously. (One of my favorite accounts is of the wife who greeted her husband with those three little words that quicken the heart of any man: "I'm in labor.")

It's hard not to love a homecoming story. But even so, many of us continue to live with unresolved conflict, unforgiveness, and bitter feelings in the relationships that mean the most. Everything that happened in the lives of Joseph and his brothers was

> *F*amily reunions are a uniquely American tradition.... They evoke a wave of nostalgia and foster a fierce affection for the place we know as home.

colored by their broken relationship. A casual observer would probably say that what was wrong between Joseph and his brothers was their fault and not his, and yet it was Joseph who initiated their reunion. The forty-fifth chapter of Genesis records five things he did to set the tone for this successful reunion, and they are things that will help you and me effect successful reunions as well.

Joseph and his family offer us a great example of a successful family reunion. The famine continued in Canaan, and the grain Joseph's brothers purchased in Egypt eventually ran out. When it did Jacob instructed his sons to return and purchase more, but they were afraid to go without Benjamin since Joseph had told them they would not see his face unless Benjamin came with them. Judah offered himself as surety for Benjamin, saying he would be responsible for Benjamin's safe return. Finally Jacob relented, but as a gesture of goodwill, he sent along with his sons some of the best products of the land of Canaan: balm, honey, aromatic gum and myrrh, pistachio nuts, and almonds. He also sent back the money Joseph returned to them on their first trip, thinking that perhaps it had been put in their grain bags by mistake.

When they arrived again in Egypt and Joseph saw Benjamin with them, he could hardly contain his joy. He commanded his servants to bring them to his house and prepare a special meal for the twelve brothers to share. (They were frightened by the invitation, thinking it was a ploy to trap them and take them for slaves. It is amazing what guilt can do to distort a man's thinking.) When they saw Joseph they gave him the presents they had brought and bowed down before him. After they exchanged pleasantries, Joseph inquired about his father and learned that he was alive and well. Then Joseph was introduced to Benjamin. He was so overwhelmed with emotion at the sight of him that he had to leave the room before his tears betrayed his identity.

When the meal was served, Joseph seated them in their exact birth order, a fact that astonished and confused them. He took food from his own table and gave it to them, but he gave Benjamin the choicest pieces and much larger amounts than the others received. They shared a wonderful meal, and when they were done, he instructed the house steward to fill their sacks with food and once again place their money in the mouth of each sack. Then he told the steward to put his silver cup in the mouth of Benjamin's sack. Joseph sent them all away at first light.

When they were just out of the city, Joseph sent the steward after them with orders to accuse them of theft and to search each man's sack. The cup, of course, was found in Benjamin's sack. They were brought back to Joseph's house, where they fell on the ground before him and offered a confession of their guilt with no excuses, not even one. There was no attempt to justify or explain. They simply said the cup had been found in their possession and that God had found out their iniquity. Then Judah stepped forward and on Benjamin's behalf gave an impassioned plea for mercy, offering himself in exchange for his younger half-brother so that Jacob's heart would not be broken. The mention of his father's name was more than Joseph could stand. He dismissed everyone but his brothers and prepared to tell them who he was. What a family reunion this would be!

He refused to publicly air "dirty laundry"

So no one stood with him while Joseph made himself known to his brothers.

Genesis 45:1

Joseph honored his brothers by providing an atmosphere of privacy for reconciliation to take place. He did not want to embarrass them by making their sins against him public. When he could not contain the truth a minute longer, he ordered everyone from the room but his brothers and began to weep with sobs so loud the entire household must have heard. What a blessed relief it must have been to look at them and say, "I am Joseph," and to be known again by his family. Instead of boldly announcing who he was, he chose to draw them to himself, saying "I am Joseph. . . . Please come near to me." Some scholars say that the Hebrew words he spoke meant more than just "get where you can see." They were words that invited intimacy. He may have opened his robe at this point so that they could see that he was circumcised, the mark of a Hebrew, not an Egyptian. His brothers were stunned by his words, but Joseph wanted them to know he wished them no harm. He wanted them to know what he had discovered years earlier: Although they *sold* him, God *sent* him, and he bore them no ill will. He tried as best he could to explain how God had again and again used his circumstances for good. And when he had said all that was on his heart, he did what he had been longing to do since the first time he saw them, he embraced and kissed them all in turn, beginning with Benjamin, and invited them to bring Jacob and come and live with him in Egypt for as long as they desired.

Joseph was wise to create an atmosphere of privacy for this moment of confrontation. When a relationship between two people is broken, it is not uncommon for one or both to go to a third party and confide their sides of the story. Often this is a serious mistake. Many times the relationship might have been quickly restored if the parties involved had not shared the details with someone else. I'm convinced that marriages could often be saved (and a lot of awkward moments avoided) if those in conflict would keep their problems to themselves for as long as possible. The involvement of a third party so often becomes a serious impediment or deterrent to the process of reconciliation.

Joseph was not looking for allies, understanding, or sympathy. He was looking for a healed relationship.

Do not misunderstand. Certainly there is a place for wise counsel in many conflicts. But privacy often provides especially fertile ground in which healing can at least begin. It takes a certain maturity to keep a grievance within appropriate boundaries.

Joseph was not looking for allies, understanding, or sympathy. He was looking for a healed relationship, and he was willing to provide the best possible climate in which that healing could take place.

He resisted the temptation to assign blame

But now, do not therefore be grieved or angry with
yourselves because you sold me here; for *God sent
me* before you to preserve life.

Genesis 45:5, italics added

Joseph chose not to use the leverage of guilt to manipulate his brothers' response to him. "I told you so" was not in his vocabulary. He did not make them sweat while he weighed their fate in his hands, nor did he read them a list of their shortcomings or their former injustices to him. Instead his first words to them were words of acceptance and understanding, not blame.

Very simply, he let them off the hook! And he did it before they even had the chance to say "I'm sorry" for what they had done. He did not punish them with aloofness or withhold his affection from them. He said he was *sent* to Egypt by his God, not *sold* there by his brothers. Can you imagine how surprised and relieved they must have been? By saying that God sent him, Joseph testified again to the pre-eminent reality of God in his life. He acknowledged that his presence in Egypt was not the result of hatred but Almighty God's plan for preservation and deliverance.

To offer forgiveness in this way requires inordinant discernment and maturity evidenced by the ability to make the right choice in a given situation. Discernment enabled Joseph to sort through the garbage from before and to salvage what was still usable in his relationship with his brothers. Perhaps he had a right to blame his brothers for what had happened to him, but he was wise enough to know that such a choice would yield him little. He was able to see beyond the immediate and to discern God's purpose, the mark of a mature man.

While living in North Carolina, I had several occasions to visit Charlotte, the "Queen City." The Myers Park section of Charlotte is an incredible maze of curving roads and cul-de-sacs, all confusing to a driver unfamiliar with the area. I soon discovered (with help from the natives) that the key to traffic

Our destiny is not controlled by powerful nations, great men, or circumstances. It rests securely and comfortably in the hands of God.

flow in Myers Park is a thoroughfare known as Providence Road. This street is the hub that runs through the section, tying together all the tangled roads.

Providence Road gets its name from Providence Church, which is located at its end. The church founders chose that name because they believed by faith that their lives were in the hands of God and His providence. Perhaps no better explanation of this idea can be found than Paul's in Romans 8:28: "And we know that all things work together for good to those who love God, to those who are the called according to His purpose." *Providence* expresses the idea that the hand of God is shaping history. We are not at the mercy of a cyclical, happenstance repetition of events or ideologies, moving aimlessly through time and space. Our destiny is not controlled by powerful nations, great men, or circumstances. It rests securely and comfortably in the hands of God. Joseph never lost his grasp of that particular truth.

He welcomed them back into his life

"Hurry and go up to my father, and say to him,
"Thus says your son Joseph: 'God has made me lord
of all Egypt; come down to me, do not tarry.'"

Genesis 45:9

Joseph took yet another step in the forgiveness process when he told his brothers to bring the entire family to Egypt to be united under his protection. Failure to take this step of inviting others back into our lives can so easily short-circuit reconciliation. He could have simply said, "It's okay. I'm not mad anymore. Go on home. You're forgiven." But would that have restored their relationship?

A **heart that has truly forgiven invites restored fellowship. It is the only heart that can.**

If we do offer words of forgiveness and acknowledge God's involvement in working our conflicts for the good, we usually stop there. It's a comfortable place to stop, because it costs us very little. At this point everyone walks away from the encounter and goes their separate ways. But there is still a strain in the relationship that is allowed to remain as we keep safe distances from one another. Joseph could have just as easily dismissed them to return to Canaan at this point, saying "If you need any more bread, just holler and I'll see that you get it. Come back for a visit when you get a chance!" Live and let live, right? But he went a step farther and said, "I want us to live together as a family again. I want us to be close." Forgiveness is rich when the injured party invites us back.

Thomas Jefferson said, "When the heart is right, the feet are swift," linking the action of our feet to the condition of our hearts. The converse of this statement is equally true. If our hearts are not right, our feet will be slow to take us to forgiveness. Do we blame God for the mate who died? The father who abused us? The spouse who left us? The child who forsook his family? A heart that has truly forgiven invites restored fellowship. It is the only heart that can.

He gave them an unexpected blessing

You shall dwell in the land of Goshen, and you shall be near to me, you and your children, your children's children, your flocks and your herds, and all that you have.

Genesis 45:10

Joseph gave his family land, and it was not a parcel no one else wanted, but the choicest land in Egypt. The gift was a serendipity, an unexpected blessing. Goshen was located on a section of the Nile River that never flooded, making it rich land for the support of goats, sheep, and other livestock.

*H*ealing a broken relationship is not a one-step process, but for the man or woman willing to go the distance, the prize is worth it.

Joseph's gift represents yet another step along the path of forgiveness. Healing a broken relationship is not a one-step process, but for the man or woman willing to go the distance, the prize is worth it. Here the relationship is sealed with a blessing, an outpouring of love and commitment that is freely given and completely undeserved.

No story illustrates this better than Jesus' parable of the prodigal son. The prodigal convinced his father to give him the portion of inheritance he would have received at his father's death, and then left for a distant country where he eventually "squandered his estate with loose living." Hungry, dirty, flat broke, and ashamed, he decided to return to his father's house and offer to be a servant, knowing he no longer deserved to be treated as a son. When he arrived home, however, an amazing thing happened. The father he had spurned greeted him with open arms, and before the apology was out of the son's mouth, his father blessed him with the gifts of a restored relationship: a robe, a ring, sandals, and a feast in his honor!

The blessing he received said, "I don't want to make you pay for what you've done. I just want us to be together again. All that I have is *still* yours, and nothing you can do will ever change that. I shall always be your father, and you shall always be my son." Such a blessing is an outward picture of what resides in the heart. Joseph felt no bitterness for his brothers, only love. Long before he had trusted God to work all things in his life for good, and learned to forgive and so live.

He took the first steps to restored fellowship

Then he fell on his brother Benjamin's neck and
wept, and Benjamin wept on his neck. Moreover
he kissed all his brothers and wept over them, and
after that his brothers talked with him.

Genesis 45:14–15

I would love to have witnessed that scene, wouldn't you? Joseph embraced each brother in turn beginning with Benjamin; then talked with them openly for the first time in twenty-five years. I believe there was a level of intimacy between them that had not existed before!

Is there anyone you are separated from today because you have been unwilling to take the first step to restore fellowship? Are you waiting for the other person to initiate the process of forgiveness? Conditional forgiveness ("Well, I'm willing to forgive them if...") is no forgiveness at all. The Bible teaches that we are to take the initiative to restore and rebuild broken relationships.

Conditional forgiveness ("Well, I'm willing to forgive them if . . .") is no forgiveness at all.

Therefore if you bring your gift to the altar, and
there remember that your brother has something
against you, leave your gift there before the altar,
and go your way. First be reconciled to your
brother, and then come and offer your gift.

Matthew 5:23–24

I Forgave You a Long Time Ago

A distant member of our family was reared in rural Mississippi and after high school attended nursing school in New Orleans. During her first year there, she began to date a young man whom she grew to love deeply. She had never really dated anyone before, but she believed this man loved her and wanted to marry her. While she was still in nursing school she became pregnant, and the man she thought loved her so much would have nothing to do with her.

She left nursing school and went to a home for unwed mothers in Natchez, Mississippi. But in order to enter the home she was required to sign a contract and agree to give up her baby for adoption shortly after it was born. Months later she gave birth to a beautiful baby girl that she was allowed to nurse and care for until the day came to give her to the adoptive parents. I'm told it took three men to hold her back as they took her baby from her. The child was adopted by a wonderful Christian couple in Ohio who named her Joy.

Joy grew into a bright, well-educated young lady and married a fine man who became a prominent record producer in Nashville, Tennessee. Through the years she had wondered about the identity of her birthmother and finally decided to try to reach her. Joy's husband spent a great deal of time and money in this pursuit, and finally his attorneys located a woman named Lizzy, who was a nurse in Mobile, Alabama. He called the hospital, identified himself, and asked if she would like to meet her daughter. Lizzy responded by saying she had long dreamed of the day this might be possible, and the three of them arranged to meet in a motel in another city.

Can you imagine the love and emotion that filled that room when this mother and daughter met? With tears streaming down her cheeks, Lizzy asked Joy if she could ever forgive her for what she had done. Joy gave her mother a long hug and said these words: "Mom, I forgave you a long time ago." Without Joy's initiative, neither she nor Lizzy would ever have known the joy of reconciliation.

The God Who Restores

The most profound words ever uttered in our universe are these: "God is good." For twenty-five years Jacob believed his son Joseph was dead. Then one day a caravan of wagons rolled along the horizon full of provisions from Egypt, goods from a far away land sent by the hand of a long lost son. Those wagons represent something that is still available to you and me today: God's provision. Imagine that God has wagons loaded with things that will meet our own particular needs and that He is longing to send them to us, no matter how far away we are.

> *The most profound words ever uttered in our universe are these: "God is good."*

Psalm 107 begins with this truth: "Oh, give thanks to the LORD, for He is good! / For His mercy endures forever." He is good, and yet His people have always found themselves in uncomfortable surroundings and in desperate need of His provision.

> They wandered in the wilderness in a desolate way....
>
> Then they cried out to the LORD in their trouble,
>
> And He delivered them out of their distresses....
>
> Those who sat in darkness and in the shadow of death,
>
> Bound in affliction and irons....

> And they drew near to the gates of death.
>
> Then they cried out to the LORD in their trouble,
>
> And He saved them out of their distresses.
>
> He sent His word and healed them. . . .
>
> He commands and raises the stormy wind,
>
> Which lifts up the waves of the sea.
>
> They mount up to the heavens,
>
> They go down again to the depths. . . .
>
> Then they cry out to the LORD in their trouble. . . .
>
> And He calms the storm.
>
> Ps. 107:4–6, 10, 13, 18–20, 25–26, 28, 29

In the desert, in the dungeon, on the deathbed, or in the deep, God answers when we cry out. And He alone is able to provide for our hearts' deepest needs. His provision plus His protection equal His providence. He *is* all we need.

You <u>Can</u> Go Home Again

This is a true story about the restoring power of a miracle-working God. The Johnsons, Biff and Sue Raye, were members of our church several years ago before moving to Denver, Colorado, where Biff finished his education. Then he and Sue Raye began working and had a daughter they named Mandy, who is now seven. Sue Raye almost died giving birth to their child and was sick a long time afterward, but this wonderful Christian family prospered and were known and loved by many.

Two years ago Biff left his wife and child, turned his back on his Christian beliefs, and went out into the world, leaving them with nothing. He indicated he no longer wanted to be a part of their Christian home, so Sue Raye called friends in Houston, and at their invitation came south. Sue Raye found a job, Mandy enrolled in school, and the two of them began a new life, living with members of our church.

Actually, there were three of them, because along with Mandy and Sue Raye came Mandy's dog, Coochi. Coochi is a mutt whose charm is rather elusive, but Mandy had just lost her dad, and she loved Coochi a lot. One Friday Sue Raye, Mandy, and Coochi drove to Beaumont (about ninety miles from Houston) to visit Sue Raye's aunt for the weekend, and Coochi somehow got out and ran away. They looked for him Friday night, then all day Saturday and Sunday. Finally they left Beaumont without Coochi, because Sue Raye had to get back to work and Mandy to school.

When she put Mandy to bed late that night, Sue Raye heard her little daughter pray: "Dear God, You're the only one who can find Coochi and bring him back to me. You know how important Coochi is. You know that I love You most of all, then I love Mommy, then Coochi, then all my friends. . . . Oh, yeah, then Daddy. So You can see how much I need Coochi now. Please bring him home." The next night she prayed, "Dear God, You're so wonderful, You're so powerful, You're such a great God. You are a loving Father and because You love me so much, please help Coochi to come home."

That night a man in Beaumont found Coochi wandering in the street. He had been lost for four days and four nights and was dirty, hungry, cold, wet, and frightened. (Coochi's not exactly a beauty even when he's cleaned up.) The man took the dog home, bathed him, and found his vaccination tag with a Denver veterinarian's phone number on it. The next morning he called Denver and spoke to the veterinarian who gave him the Johnsons' name and two telephone numbers. His second long-distance call was to their home number, which had been disconnected. Then he called Biff's office and learned that he no longer worked there, but they gave him the number of someone who might know where Sue Raye and Mandy were staying in Houston.

Phone call number four was to the home of a friend in Denver who happened to be an assistant football coach for the Denver Broncos. His wife gave the man Sue Raye's work number in Houston. After five long-distance phone calls, he found Sue Raye and let her know that Coochi was safe and sound. She and Mandy waited until Friday to drive back to Beaumont and pick up the dog, but Sue Raye wanted to be back in church Sunday morning. Our sermon text was Psalm 107, a passage of scripture she had clung to all summer, because she said, "I felt like I was in a desert, in a dungeon, and on my deathbed all the time."

If the story had ended there, it would still have been wonderful, but it didn't. Saturday while Sue Raye and Mandy were in Beaumont, Biff called Houston to talk to Sue Raye. He got the number in Beaumont, called there, and according to Sue Raye, cried. For the first time in a long time, he sounded like himself. He said, "I want you to forgive me. I want to come back home. I want to get things right with our family, but I don't know what to do." Biff did not have the money to come to see Sue Raye and Mandy, but a friend in Denver gave him a one-way plane ticket to Houston. He left that night.

Before the first worship service the next morning, I asked Sue Raye and Mandy if we could share their story and let our congregation meet Coochi. (I understand he got a special hair-do for the occasion.) They agreed, and Sue Raye and Biff also agreed to go public with the rest of the story as well. (Mandy had still not seen her dad and did not know he had returned.) After Sue Raye, Mandy, and Coochi came up to the platform, Biff joined them. It was an unforgettable moment for all of us.

We have an amazing God, don't we? Beginning with a mutt named Coochi, He brought this broken family back to the point where healing could begin. Mandy believed that He cared about her dog and could bring him home, and He did. But He didn't stop there. It's been a tough road for the Johnsons, and there are scars from the past that may never go away, but they are healing, because our God is a God who restores. He *is* good.

Restoration

Everyone reading this book could say at some point in their lives, "I know what it's like to be in a desert. I've been in a dry place. I've been thirsty. I've been lost." "I know about the dungeon. I've felt like a captive. I'm in chains now and don't know when I'll get out of this place." Others might say, "I've been on my deathbed. I thought I was dying and wanted to. I couldn't eat. I couldn't sleep." Some would say, "I've been out in the depths. I'm out beyond my capacity to swim. I'm sick and tired and staggering through life like I'm drunk, not knowing which way to turn."

*G*od wants to bring you out. He wants to deliver you. He wants to provide for you, make a home for you, give you hope.

God wants to bring you out. He wants to deliver you. He wants to provide for you, make a home for you, give you hope. More than anything, He wants to gather you to Himself. That's what God is like, and He will never be any other way. There's an old saying, "Home is where the heart is." Joseph knew the secret that kept him "falling uphill" throughout his life: The heart that knows the reality of God's presence is always at home with Him.

Reconciliation

- Reconciliation is easiest in an atmosphere of privacy. Privacy honors the guilty party by showing him respect and allowing healing to begin.
- Pointing fingers and assigning blame is a useless exercise if reconciliation is the goal. Resist the urge to make the guilty party sweat—it's counterproductive!

- Discernment allows us to distinguish between throw-away and usable ingredients of a relationship. What we have a right to do may not be what is best.
- Forgiveness without an invitation to restoration is not genuine forgiveness.
- Initiative is the key to real reconciliation. Don't wait for someone else to initiate what you know is right.

Chapter 12

Immanuel

God with Us

Then Israel said to Joseph, "Behold, I am dying, but God will be with you and bring you back to the land of your fathers."

Genesis 48:21

Behold, the virgin shall be with child, and bear a Son, and they shall call His name Immanuel, which is translated, "God with us."

Matthew 1:23

Immanuel

Last words are precious commodities. Attorneys construct their closing arguments in court as carefully as military generals plan an invasion. Every word must count. Deathbed declarations may contain truths that a lifetime of conversation never once revealed. Knowing that the time for talk will soon be over makes every word significant.

After Joseph and his brothers were reconciled in Egypt, he sent them home with the invitation to return with their father, Jacob, so they could live comfortably with him in Egypt for the rest of their lives.

When Jacob received the news that Joseph was alive, he set out with all his might for Egypt so that he could see him again before he died. God spoke to Jacob on the way and eased his fears, saying, "Do not fear to go down to Egypt, for I will make you a great nation there." When Pharaoh learned of the family's arrival from Canaan, and that they were shepherds by trade, he gave them the land of Goshen to settle and put them in charge of his livestock.

Jacob lived well in Egypt for seventeen years and died there when he was 147 years old. His last request to Joseph before his death was that he be buried not in Egypt, but in Canaan with his fathers. Joseph promised to honor that request. As he approached his last days, he called Joseph and the rest of his family to his side. Joseph watched him embrace and bless his own sons, Ephraim and Manasseh, laying his right hand on Ephraim, the younger, and his left hand on Manasseh. Then he blessed Joseph with these words: "Behold, I am dying, but *God will be with you* and bring you back to the land of your fathers" (Gen. 48:21, italics added). They did return, seventy family members in all, and lived out their days in the land of Goshen.

*T*here is no promise more assuring than the promise of a father's presence. Knowing that we are not alone can bolster our courage like nothing else.

However he might have failed earlier in the fathering department, Jacob's last words about the presence of God affirmed a truth Joseph had experienced so many times throughout his life. "God will be with you," Jacob assured Joseph, "and bring you back to the land of your fathers." Even though Joseph knew the reality of this promise from his own experiences, it must have been a comfort to hear from his earthly father that he would not be alone and would one day be home! Egypt was a temporary dwelling place for Joseph and the sons of Jacob, but one day their offspring would return to Canaan. These were Jacob's last words to the son he loved best.

There is no promise more assuring than the promise of a father's presence. Knowing that we are not alone can bolster our courage like nothing else. And knowing that we're going home gives us security and even patience to dwell temporarily in strange, unsettling places. Joseph knew this even better than Jacob did, because he had *been* in the far-away places and felt the presence of God there throughout his life.

"God will be with you." He had been . . . always—through the death of Joseph's mother, conflict in their home, tension with his brothers, through slavery and imprisonment, through false accusations and forgotten promises, God had been with Joseph.

Although there were times when He seemed far away, Joseph never doubted His presence. Joseph learned that the reality of God's presence has very little to do with how a person feels. To hear in his father's blessing the very truth that his life had revealed must have been so affirming. His promise was not only that God would be with Joseph, but that He would eventually take him back to the land of his fathers.

Joseph's life was full of strife, misfortune, and heartache, and his family was the source of most of his pain. (It's true that the only ones who can hurt us are the ones we love.) His story is a thoroughly contemporary picture of the things that go wrong in families today. But he was loved, and he never lost the reality of God's presence in his life.

Have you been kissed and tucked in? Is God real in your life? Through Joseph God held together the family of Jacob, and through Jacob's twelve sons the twelve tribes of Israel were established. Then in the fullness of time, a son came through the tribe of Judah and the house of David to Mary and Joseph. His name was Jesus, and before His birth God appeared to Joseph, saying, "Behold, the virgin shall be with child, and bear a Son, and they shall call His name Immanuel, which is translated, *God with us*" (Matt. 1:23).

The same promise Jacob gave to Joseph on his deathbed, God gives us—He will be with us in the person of His Son, Jesus Christ.

God with us! The same promise Jacob gave to Joseph on his deathbed, God gives us—He will be with us in the person of His Son, Jesus Christ. The same power that sustained Joseph through his darkest days and brought about the restoration of his family is available to us as well. He will be with us, and His presence is life-changing!

I'm Okay Now . . . God Is Here with Me

Desmond and his family lived at the Star of Hope mission in Houston, a temporary shelter for the homeless of our city. Last summer our high school young people served as workers and counselors at a camp where the children of the families who live at the mission get to spend a week in the country. Desmond was an inquisitive little guy of seven, who listened intently to the words of his counselors as they talked about Jesus and what it means to know Him. He was full of questions. "If God is real big, how big is His big toe?" "If God is everywhere at once, what part of Him is in our cabin?" (Children can be refreshingly literal, can't they?)

Desmond's counselor Ray said that he was the most intense child in their cabin—he really listened and tried to understand all that was being said. Desmond was curious about God and how He could be everywhere at once. He was amazed by the concept of a God who is right here with us. Each night before lights out, Desmond would ask Ray to sit by his bed until he fell asleep. Most of the other kids fell into their bunks exhausted at the end of a long day, but Desmond was never ready for the lights to go out and did not want to be alone in the dark.

The last night of camp the counselors talked to the kids about asking Jesus to come and live inside their hearts. Desmond knew this was something he wanted, and he talked to Ray about it. Ray explained to him what it means to be a Christian, and the two of them prayed for Desmond to receive Christ. When they finished praying, Desmond looked up and said, "Ray, I'm a Christian!" (Then he went inside the cabin, turned the lights back on, and enthusiastically announced it to the other campers and counselors!)

That night as he climbed in bed, again he asked Ray to come and sit with him until he fell asleep. Ray reminded Desmond that he needn't be afraid of the dark or being alone anymore, because now that he was a Christian, God was always with him. Just the same, Desmond said, he'd appreciate Ray sitting by his bed for just a little while. So Ray settled in next to the bunk, and Desmond shut his eyes. Little by little his body began to relax and his breathing grew calm. After five minutes he opened his eyes, in the dark, looked at his friend, and said, "Ray, I'm okay now . . . God is here with me."

The Father's Everlasting Presence

Immanuel—God with us, the presence of a Father who loves us with an everlasting love. This was the stronghold of Joseph's life, and it is the stronghold of ours. Maybe you were kissed and tucked in as a child. Maybe not. But regardless of your family background or the circumstances of your life, you have been loved, and you can know the presence of God. God loves you and wants you to experience peace and to have abundant life. The Bible says, "We have peace with God through our Lord Jesus Christ" (Rom. 5:1). Jesus is the way to that kind of peace, and He alone offers abundant life. In fact that is the reason He gives in John 10:10 for His coming into the world: "I have come that they may have life, and that they may have it more abundantly."

*R*egardless of your family background or the circumstances of your life, you have been loved, and you can know the presence of God.

Peace and abundant life are what God wants for us, but we miss those gifts when we choose to disobey Him and go our own ways. The choice to disobey Him is called sin, and it separates us from God and the things He wants to give us. The Bible says, "For all have sinned and fall short of the glory of God" (Rom. 3:23). The end of sin is death, and nothing that we can do on our own can free us from its grip. No matter what we try—good works, religion, wisdom, clean living—we can never be good enough for a holy and perfect God. Every effort, every human mechanism we have access to falls short of what He intends for us.

Desmond found out about God's solution to our sin problem. The solution is a person, and His name is Jesus. Jesus Christ, the only Son of God, died on a cross and paid the penalty for our sin so that we could have an unbroken relationship with God. This was part of His plan for us: "For God so loved the world that He gave His only begotten Son, that whoever believes in Him should not perish but have everlasting life" (John 3:16). No matter who we are or what we have done, the offer is good: "But God demonstrates His own love toward us, in that while we were still sinners, Christ died for us" (Rom. 5:8).

How do we get into the presence of God? We get there by responding to the invitation of His Son Jesus, who says, "Behold, I stand at the door and knock. If anyone hears My voice and opens the door, I will come in to him and dine with him, and he with Me" (Rev. 3:20). All we have to do is ask: "If you confess with your mouth the Lord Jesus and believe in your heart that God has raised Him from the dead, you will be saved. For with the heart one believes unto righteousness, and with the mouth confession is made unto salvation" (Rom. 10:9–10).

Are you spiritually and eternally kissed and tucked in? Do you rest easily in the presence of a Father who loves you so that you are fully equipped to meet the challenges of life head-on? Nothing that the world can put in your way is bigger than the One who walks with you. If you have known the security of a loving family, you know something of the kind of love I'm talking about. And if you have not experienced this kind of loving security, get ready! There is hope and joy available to you that is beyond anything you could imagine. God will be a Father to you if you will only ask Him.

There is hope and joy available to you that is beyond anything you could imagine. God will be a Father to you if you will only ask Him.

Parents, are your children kissed and tucked in? Do they know the security of a loving family? Is their understanding of God helped by their images of their own father and mother? Yours is the opportunity of a lifetime. The birth of the nation of Israel was a family affair, and God's desire was for a covenant people who would bear a family resemblance to Him and be a light to a godless world. A family today that loves one another, works together, plays together, and worships together is a beacon in our darkening world as well. No matter what difficulties your family may face, God's presence can be just as real to you as it was to Joseph thousands of years ago.

In his book *The Power of a Purpose,* Nenien McPherson denies the myth of "greener grass," saying that too many of us live "if only" lives: "If only I had married someone else." "If only my children were better." "If only I had chosen a different career." "If only my parents had been more loving." The truth is that changing other people and changing our environment are not the solutions we so often believe them to be. We can change wives or husbands, change jobs, change cities, or even change our names—all to no avail.

Joseph seemed to find green grass wherever he was: in a pit, in prison, in a rich man's household, or in a king's palace. He refused to play the blame game and chose to believe in God's presence and providence in every situation.

Egypt was rich and wild and bountiful, and the opportunities for Joseph were incredible. But he never forgot his home, its sights and smells and sounds, and he never stopped longing to return to it some day. Away from the place that God created for us, we are all homesick. And the promise that He will one day return us to that place has to be the richest blessing He could bestow.

"We can drift along from place to place and keep looking over the fence for green pastures," says McPherson, "but *every one of them* has brown spots, cockleburs and beggar-lice. There is no green grass, except as our vision, courage, commitment, and hard work make the grass grow green wherever we are and with whomever we may be."[1]

I do not know the unique challenges your particular family faces today, but I am convinced that they are best met as Joseph met his: in the presence and power of God the Father. He has given you and me this promise—"I will be with you; I will not fail you or forsake you. Be strong and courageous. . . ."

Notes

CHAPTER 1

1. Amy Carmichael, *Toward Jerusalem*, First American Edition (Ft. Washington, PA: The Christian Litereature Crusade, 1977). Used by permission.

CHAPTER 2

1. Moss Hart, *Act One* (New York: The Modern Library, 1959), 24–25.

CHAPTER 6

1. Stephen R. Covey, *The 7 Habits of Highly Effective People* (New York: Fireside, 1989), 108.

CHAPTER 7

1. John White, *Eros Defiled* (Downers Grove, IL: InterVarsity Press, 1977), 77.
2. C. S. Lewis, *The Four Loves* (New York: Harcourt Brace Jovanovich, 1960), 10.
3. Ibid., 106.
4. Willard F Harley, Jr., *His Needs, Her Needs* (Old Tappan, NJ: Revell, 1986), 10.
5. J. Allan Petersen, *The Myth of the Greener Grass* (Wheaton, IL: Tyndale, 1983), 202.

CHAPTER 8

1. William J. Gaither, "Something Beautiful" (CCLI 166883, J & J Publishing). Used by permission.
2. Emily Dickinson, untitled. *Emily Dickinson Collected Poems* (Philadelphia, PA: Running Press Book Publishers, 1991), 100.
3. Charles Spurgeon, *Twelve Sermons on Prayer* (Grand Rapids, MI: Baker Book House, 1971), 56.

CHAPTER 10

1. William Shakespeare, *Macbeth*, Act V, Scene II.

CHAPTER 12

1. Nenien McPherson, *The Power of a Purpose* (Old Tappan, NJ: Revell, 1959)', 47–48.

About the Author

Dr. Ed Young was born and raised in Laurel, Mississippi, and attended the University of Alabama and Mississippi College. Challenged by an athiest and fellow student at the University of Alabama who questioned his commitment to God, Dr. Young began to seriously seek God's purpose for his life. Six months later he surrendered to the call to preach the gospel and enrolled in Mississippi College to continue his education.

Following graduation from Mississippi College, he married his long-time friend and sweetheart, Jo Beth Landrum, and continued his education at Southeastern Seminary. He holds academic degrees from Southeastern (B.D.), Furman University (D.D.), Criswell Center for Biblical Studies (D.D.), Southwest Baptist University (S.T.D.), Mississippi College (D.D.), and Hannibal-LaGrange College (D.D.)

Before becoming a pastor of Second Baptist Church, Houston, Texas, in 1978, Dr. Young served as pastor of First Baptist Church, Erwin, North Carolina; First Baptist Church, Canton, North Carolina; First Baptist Church, Taylors, South Carolina; and First Baptist Church, Columbia, South Carolina. Dr. Young was elected President of the Southern Baptist Convention in June of 1992, and re-elected to a second term in 1993. In his years at Second Baptist Church, "The Fellowship of Excitement" has seen phenomenal growth. It is currently one of the largest and fastest-growing congregations in America and has been the focus of recent national and international media attention from *The Wall Street Journal, USA Today,* NBC, CBS, and the British Broadcasting Corporation. In 1991 Second Baptist led all Southern Baptist churches in baptisms with over one thousand.

Dr. and Mrs. Young have three sons. Ed is married to the former Lisa Lee and is pastor of the Los Colinas Baptist Church in Irving, Texas. Ben is married to the former Elliott Carter and is minister to single adults at Second Baptist Church, Houston. Their youngest son, Cliff, is a college student and a musician. Dr. and Mrs. Young have a granddaughter, Lee Beth, and a grandson, E.J., born to Ed and Lisa.